CW00321851

# HELEN MIRREN

## In the Frame

### My Life in Words and Pictures

WEIDENFELD & NICOLSON

# Contents

# *Introduction*

**I must have started** about twenty journals in my life. One, written at the age of fourteen and reproduced in this book, ambitiously calls itself 'Chapter 1 Volume 1'. It lasted for all of three pages. It is unbelievably boring. No natural writer then.

Some journals I started at the beginning of a job, a film or a play, others were inspired by finding myself somewhere foreign and remarkable. But no matter how fascinating the experience, the journals have invariably been abandoned. I have more interest in living the life than recording it.

In spite of being able to memorise reams of dialogue, I have a blissfully forgetful brain. This can be a great advantage in marriage – one of the many things that holds us together is that my husband can tell me the same story many times and each time I listen enthralled and laugh genuinely at the right moments, having forgotten that he has told me before – but such forgetfulness is less of an asset when it comes to journaling.

Working in the theatre, and loving its transitory nature ('carving in ice', as it was once described to me, for a theatre performance survives only in the memory of the audience who saw it), made me want to let go of things. I have never been a hoarder of cherished programmes, photos and stage memorabilia. Luckily my mother – proud, of course – kept mementoes, as did many of my friends who kindly lent material for this book.

When I read an autobiography, I am always drawn to the pictures. To me, it is what lies behind a photograph that makes it interesting. As you read and discover more about the personalities involved, the photos become more telling. The body language, the clothes, the background all take on a far greater meaning, and I find myself returning to the same photo again and again.

As an actor, gestures and body language are tools of the trade. You are always wondering what is behind a smile or a frown, or why someone's hat is worn like that, and what is that hand doing in that pocket? You search for something you can just perceive though it is not fully in the consciousness, in other words, what is on the edge of your vision: a form, a shape, a feeling, a fear, a pleasure … a something.

So here I give you some pictures from my life, and I try to talk around the picture, towards the wonderful parade of people, places, work and experiences that constitute some of my life. I ask those who have shared my life with me in the living of it to forgive me if they remember it differently. Memories are slippery things, and liable to transmute.

I am not interested in psychological excavations, except where acting is concerned. I have always found the world outside myself of more interest than the world within. Perhaps that comes of the way I was brought up. My mother would check 'thank you' letters to make sure the word 'I' only appeared once, and she'd cross out all references to myself. She thought it was boring or tasteless to talk about yourself. Of course, I now will write about myself for many pages.

Part of my job as an actress is to do interviews, but while I find it easy to talk about the work, I tend to frustrate interviewers by avoiding talking about myself. For the same reason I have never been to a shrink.

Actually, I lie; I did go to a shrink once. When I was about twenty-three I was very unhappy and, yes, self-obsessed and insecure. It seems to me that the years between eighteen and twenty-eight are the hardest, psychologically. It's then you realise this is make or break, you no longer have the excuse of youth, and it is time to become an adult – but you are not ready. I just could not believe that anything I desired would happen, and the responsibility of making my own way, economically, artistically and emotionally, was terrifying. So I went to a psychologist.

Now I don't know whether he did this on purpose, realising that all I needed to do was grow up, but after I had poured out my unhappiness to him, the psychologist very, very quietly, in a strong Scottish accent, began to explain to me the root cause and solution to my misery. I could not understand a word. I asked him if he wouldn't mind repeating it. He did, and I still couldn't understand a word. The fourth time of asking I gave up, and realised that an analyst was not going to work for me.

My next stop on this journey of self-discovery was to visit a hand reader. Though I've never been a believer in astrology or the art of reading palms, I was pretty desperate and he came highly recommended. So I made my way to a nondescript house in a back street of Golders Green and went into the dingy, very ordinary living room where he did his readings. He was an Indian man, more like an accountant than a mystic. I liked him. He handed me cheap paper and a pencil, saying, 'I will study your hand and then I will speak very fast. You will not remember what I will say, so write it down as fast as you can.' And that was exactly what happened. He spent about ten minutes intensely studying my hand, I can't remember which one, and then he began to speak. I had to write so fast I could not take stock of what he was saying. After about twenty minutes, I was a fiver poorer and back on the street with my whole future life spelt out in scrawling script on a massive heap of paper. It was quite true, I could not remember any of it. Well, there is one thing I remember. He said, 'You will be successful in life, but you will see your greatest success later, after the age of forty-five.'

Not something you want to hear at the age of twenty-three, but it turned out he was right.

At least it brought to an end my period of desperate introspection and miserable self-obsession. As I looked at those scrawled pages, I realised that I did not want to know what the future held. I wanted my life to be an adventure. Whatever pleasure or pains, successes or failures, disasters or triumphs were waiting for me, I wanted them to come as a surprise.

I took the pages and stuffed them into the first rubbish bin I could find, then stepped out into the rest of my life.

# Russia

## *My father's Russian ancestry*

**In the house** where I grew up in Leigh-on-Sea there was an old wooden trunk in the basement that had belonged to my grandfather. It was full of tools and paint pots sat on top of it. Scarred with age and dribbles of paint, it was just possible to make out some Cyrillic writing on the side. When my mother died and the house came to be sold, I took the trunk, emptied out the tools and filled its cedar interior with Grandpa's papers, a yellowing collection of letters written in a tiny, spidery Russian hand, and pages typed on the Cyrillic typewriter Grandpa had brought from Russia, with mysterious diagrams and maps. Somehow these papers had survived my mother's periodic clear-outs. After shoving them in the trunk, I forgot about them for another ten years.

My grandfather, Pyotr Vassili Mironov, was a proud and loyal member of the Czarist army. In Russia the military class was a whole social structure of its own. Grandpa was a proud and loyal member of that class, coming from military families on both sides. His mother, Countess Kamensky, had married outside the aristocracy, to Vassili Pyotr Mironov (the first-born son of each generation was always given the same two forenames, with the order changing from one generation to the next), a very successful military man. As the beloved (and undoubtedly very spoilt) only son in a family of seven, it was inevitable that Grandfather would join the army. He served in that brutal Russo-Japanese War of 1904, where the Russians were underarmed and suffered horrible losses. In 1916, having risen rapidly in rank, he was selected to join a small delegation

My grandfather, resplendent and proud in his Czarist military uniform, complete with medals from his service in the Russo-Japanese war.

sent to buy military supplies from the British. To begin with, Pyotr and his family were honoured guests of the British government, living in luxurious quarters within the Russian embassy and enjoying comfort befitting representatives of the Czar; my father attended private school in London. But then came the Bolshevik Revolution, which contrary to Grandpa's strongly held belief that the people loved the Czar too much for revolution ever to take hold, was not about to go away.

Pyotr's pride in nation had prevented him bringing anything from Russia except his typewriter, pictures of the Czar and Czarina, a few pre-revolutionary roubles and his wooden military trunk, made for him on the family estate. As a result, post Revolution, the family were left with no means of support. The only way my grandfather, with his halting, heavily accented English, could earn money was in the time-honoured way of immigrants: as a taxi driver. So the proud, nationalistic, loyal Pyotr Vassili Mironov, descendant of the noble Kamenskys, instead of inheriting the family's Kuryanovo estates in Russia, became a London cabbie in order to

Pages from one of my grandfather's letters, kept for years in an old wooden trunk.

support his wife and children. My father had no choice but to finish his education early and make his own way in the world.

In those post-revolutionary years Grandpa's mother and sisters wrote to him. Their letters are painful in their careful and stoic descriptions of the deprivations of the Russian people. Then, at the height of the Stalinist purges, it obviously became too dangerous to write, and the letters stopped coming. From 1931 to the 1950s there were no letters, and then a flood.

These were the elegantly handwritten letters that came to reside, along with Pyotr's memoirs, in the trunk I inherited. Their revelations remained hidden for many years.

It was a question of finding a translator . . .

Then, as these things happen, a flurry of activity. Simon and Olga Geoghan did amazing work on those magical letters and Roger Silverman beautifully translated the memoirs. At last my sister and I were launched on a voyage of discovery that is not over yet.

The latest chapter has been the incredible discovery, thanks to the work of a researcher called Will Stewart, of a cache of letters from my grandfather, together with pictures of myself and my family, that had been hidden away in the Moscow apartment of a distant relative.

# Mironov Family Tree

## Here we all are...

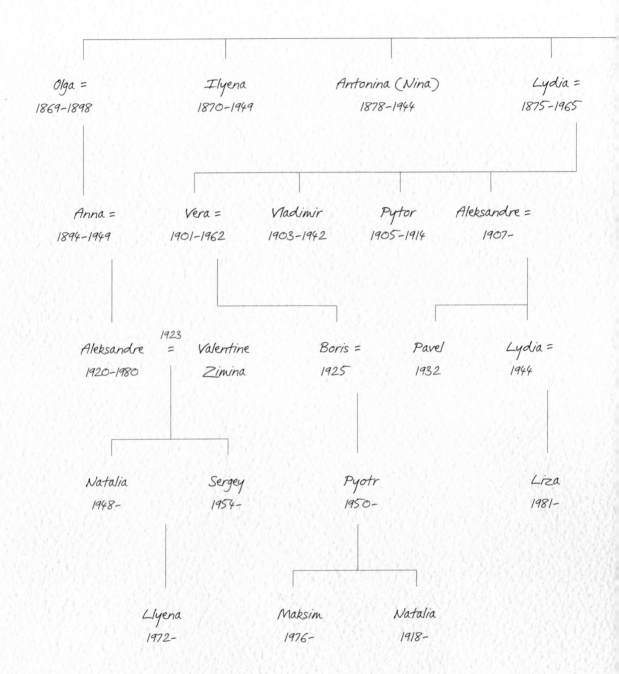

Olga =
1869-1898

Ilyena
1870-1949

Antonina (Nina)
1878-1944

Lydia =
1875-1965

Anna =
1894-1949

Vera =
1901-1962

Vladimir
1903-1942

Pytor
1905-1914

Aleksandre =
1907-

Aleksandre
1920-1980

1923
=

Valentine
Zimina

Boris =
1925

Pavel
1932

Lydia =
1944

Natalia
1948-

Sergey
1954-

Pyotr
1950-

Liza
1981-

Llyena
1972-

Maksim
1976-

Natalia
1918-

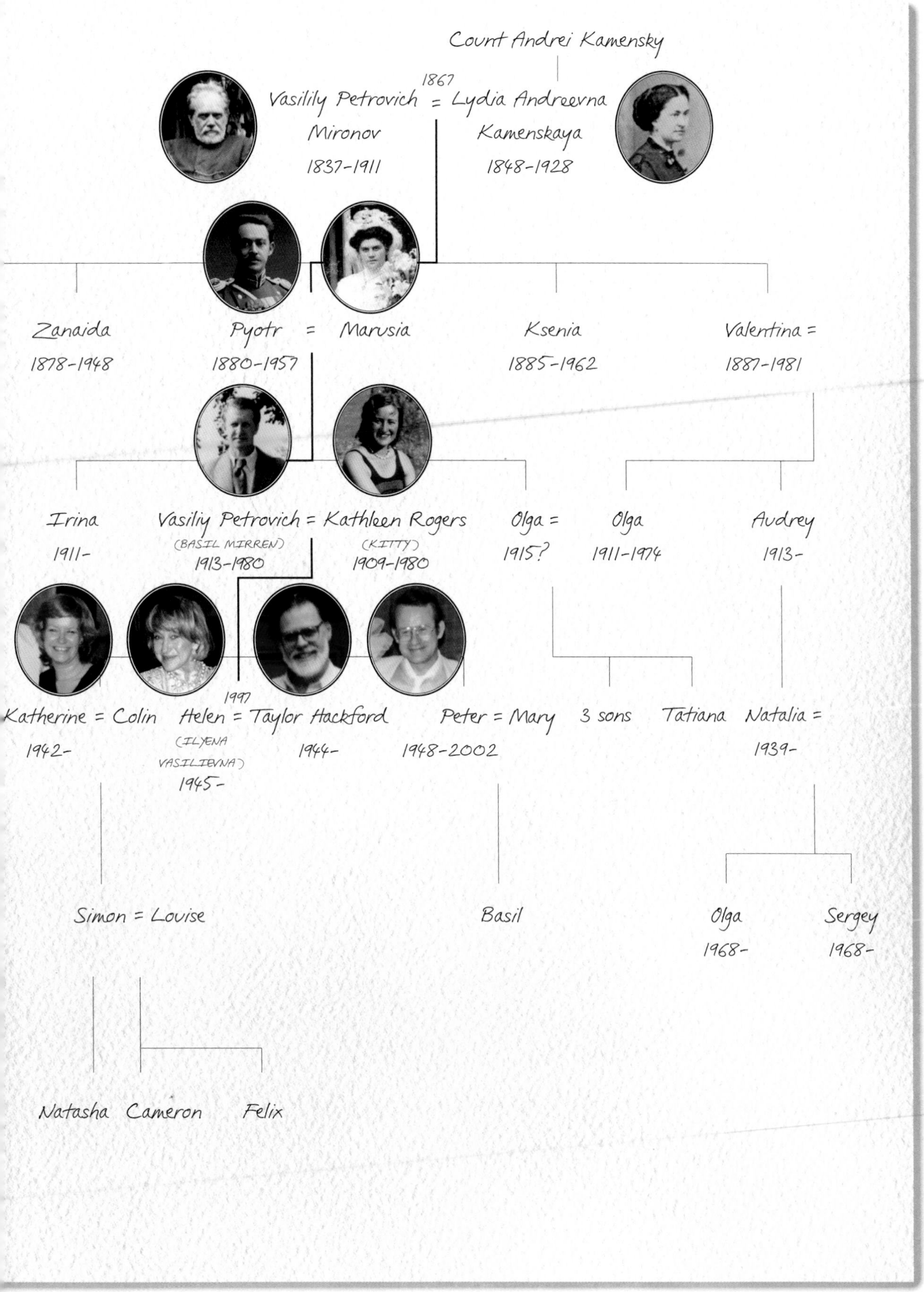

Count Andrei Kamensky

1867
Vasiliy Petrovich = Lydia Andreevna
Mironov         Kamenskaya
1837–1911       1848–1928

Zanaida          Pyotr  =  Marusia          Ksenia              Valentina =
1878–1948       1880–1957                   1885–1962           1887–1981

Irina     Vasiliy Petrovich = Kathleen Rogers    Olga =    Olga      Audrey
1911–     (BASIL MIRREN)      (KITTY)             1915?     1911–1974  1913–
          1913–1980           1909–1980

                                        1997
Katherine = Colin  Helen = Taylor Hackford   Peter = Mary   3 sons   Tatiana   Natalia =
1942–              (ILYENA                    1948–2002                          1939–
                   VASILIEVNA)     1944–
                   1945–

Simon = Louise                      Basil                            Olga      Sergey
                                                                     1968–     1968–

Natasha  Cameron    Felix

The picture on the right was in my
grandfather's trunk. The rest, taken on the same
day, were found in Russia ninety years later. They
show my grandfather with his sisters and friends,
larking about in the snow on their family estates,
unaware of the impending revolution. I love these
pictures, which are so very Chekhovian.

Left: A picture of
my grandfather with
his fiancée, my grand-
mother, and his sisters
and their friends, in
the summertime.

Above: My great aunts.
Right: My great-grandmother.

These remarkable pictures were also found in Russia, filling in a gap in my knowledge of my family roots. My grandfather is shown with his father, a friend, a sister, a servant and an unknown little girl. They are sitting on the veranda of their house at Kuryanovo, which lies between Smolensk and Moscow.

These photographs also were found in Moscow in 2007.
I was astounded to see pictures of my grandparents' wedding.

Top left: My grandparents as a young married couple.
Above: Before the arrival of my father, with their first child, Irina.
Top right: My father, Basil Mirren, with sister Irina.

Here is my father, on the right, as the spoilt young scion of an illustrious Russian family, destined at this point, I am sure, to serve the Czar of the future and tend the family estate. His actual destiny was very different. This picture is moving to me. Years later one of his aunts, now trapped in Stalinist Russia, writes of him at this age, learning to walk, holding on to the furniture in Kuryanovo.

# *Excerpts from the Russian letters*

## 1917

*The worsening economic situation is the cause of a lot of grief. But then who isn't suffering at the moment? Russia's position is endlessly difficult. I won't go into more detail about the latest events in the country because I want to be certain that this letter gets through to you. Uncle Sergey is in the reserves, Ninov is here in Petrograd and I am planning to pay him a visit in the next few days. All these events are literally worrying your mother to death. You yourself know that for her the destruction of Kuryanovo would be the destruction of her life's work and all her future plans. For the moment Kuryanovo hasn't been the target of any outrages, but all the newspapers carry such terrible stories that it is too painful to bear. If something were to happen in Kuryanovo it would undoubtedly kill her.*

## 1921

*Write in more detail, my dear — what are you doing? How do you earn enough money for your everyday living expenses? One needs so much money for a family and your army service finished on 1 May 1918! Three and a half years ago! It's frightful to think of you in a foreign land without any work and it's very hard for me not being able to help you, my priceless Petrusya. But however difficult my separation from you is, I would never ask you to come over here, my darling, you must act as you see fit …*

## 1928

*My heart will always be open to you and feels the pain of every sadness that you suffer. Always remember this. I know that you don't like to write letters but this is not so important, you only need to know that when you write your voice is heard with great joy and that you are remembered with great fondness. I kiss you with all my strength, my dear Petrusyenka, and mingle my tears with yours.*
*Valya*

## 1928

*My dear Petrusya,*
*I am no longer capable of writing to you myself. I have just had my photograph taken and I send two of them to you and to Vava. May God grant you happiness and success and may He protect you from all misfortune. God has graced you with energy and a robust spirit. God has not granted you happiness in your married life but has granted you great joy in your children — and I assure you that this is a great happiness indeed. I experience this happiness every hour. Farewell, my dear. For the last time I ask you to forgive me for any offences I might have given. I had a feeling a while back that we would never see each other again in this world. May God be with you, my dear.*
*I kiss you.*
*Your ever loving Mama*

## 1928

*At ten o'clock Mama's breathing became more and more intermittent and she opened her eyes. Vera read the Last Rites and Mama's eyes were turned towards her, then Valya carried on reading them and Mama's eyes moved towards her. She was getting increasingly short of breath. At ten forty-five Mama's suffering ended and she finally left us. She was surrounded by all her children, the only people who weren't there were you and Nina.*

*Mama was buried at the Vagankovskoye Cemetery — only Communists are allowed to be buried at Novodevichy Cemetery now …*

The Mironov family house, Kuryanovo, in the depths of a Russian winter before the Revolution.

## 1928

*The lime alley was still there. In the park and in the fir groves only the largest firs suitable for building purposes had been cut down. The timber cooperative chopped them down, cut them into large logs and sold most of them in Moscow. In Moscow there is a terrible housing shortage. Therefore many of those who work in Moscow live all year round in dachas outside the city. As a result these dacha villages are growing at a frightful rate. Of course some of the trees were stolen as well. The grain harvest failed this year and all those who can have moved to Moscow. As you probably know the house fell down a long time ago … it had become a wilderness, littered with chunks of masonry and bricks. On the site where the house had been was a large mound overgrown with nettles.*

*There weren't even any traces of the old garden paths but a few of the rose bushes had fought their way through the undergrowth. I dug up one bush from the large garden – this was the pink rose – and one from the front garden where side flower beds used to be – this was the white rose … We went through the park and saw that all the large fir trees had been cut down. We reached the red gates. The threshing house is no longer there but the drying barn is still standing. In the park at the beginning of the lime tree alley on what used to be our croquet lawn a potato clamp has been dug out. Mama's garden is now quite overgrown but the apple trees are still there and you can still make out the blackcurrant bushes. To this day no one has done anything to look after this garden. Not one of our animals is left. We were told that in the spring the cows, horses and sheep were taken away to Samoilovo. I was left with a very sad impression. The fields, forests and environs were all so familiar but the estate itself seemed alien and quite dilapidated.*

# Dad

*Changing from Mironov to Mirren*

**My father had a good education**; for a while he attended a private boarding school, but had to leave early – I suppose because the money ran out. He was also musical and as a young man made his living playing the viola. Some of my earliest memories are of my father playing Bruch on his viola, though he was no longer a professional musician by that time, the Second World War having put an end to that career.

He was vehemently anti-Nazi in his youth. Very much in opposition to his Czarist father, he became a socialist and even took part in the anti-Mosley demonstrations in the East End. His account of the famous Cable Street 'Riot' is reproduced here:

Battle of Cable Street, 4 October 1936
*There was no anti-fascist procession, just 250,000 people, mostly local dockers and Jews, blocking the roads. Barricades were built by furniture being thrown out of windows. This I saw myself. I was there because I belonged to the TGWU.*

*The Communist cell met before Branch meetings and decided on the line to take, and we were urged to go independently to Commercial Road.*

*Information was given to the crowd by word of mouth.*

*When I was in Cable Street someone shouted, 'They are going down [illegible] Street! We ran there and when I got there the fascists were passing, men, women and children in uniform, with a double row of police on either side. The anti-fascist crowd thickened to about four deep on my side. I got a violent blow on the head, and thought I had been attacked by the crowd. I was tall and young and I may have looked like a plain-clothes policeman. Then I saw a silver cigarette case on the ground; someone must have thrown it and this was what hit me. One of the crowd picked it up.*

*The opposition was not physical confrontation. It was thought we could argue and convince. When the fascists proposed to march through the East End, in full strength, the idea was to block their way by filling the streets, not to fight the police. It was a form of passive resistance. Aggression came from the fascists and the police.*

*At that time the majority in Britain were neutral or sympathetic to fascism abroad. Order instead of chaos. Persecution of the Jews was not believed.*

He wanted to fight but, whether for medical reasons or because he was a 'foreigner', he was not allowed to join the services. Instead he drove an ambulance throughout the war, thus saving lives rather than taking them. Serving in the East End during the Blitz brought him into contact with the terrible suffering endured by Londoners.

It was in the East End that he met my mother. Before the war, they both worked in the depot of Jacqmar Fabrics, a high-end supplier of materials to posh ladies and their dressmakers. He was five years younger than her, but he was madly in love and romanced her by taking her to the first Italian and Greek restaurants in London. In fact, to my great delight one of these restaurants, Bertorelli's, is miraculously still there in Charlotte Street. My parents always remembered Bertorelli's as the location where they fell in love. Today it is not considered remotely exotic to eat Italian food, but in 1939 Britain was a class-ridden, arrogantly xenophobic, overcooked-beef-and-cabbage-eating world. To eat foreign food, and date a Russian émigré five years younger than herself – let alone marry him – must have been a brave individualistic act for a West Ham-born working-class girl.

Dad at home in Leigh-on-Sea.

My father, and I warn you, here follows an unobjective love letter, was the kindest and best of men. In his early years, as an émigré with a strange name, I think he always felt an outsider, uncomfortable in a country that was at that time very homogeneous. Excluded by his foreignness and also by his politics, and much to the frustration and despair of my mother, he rejected a self-interested pursuit of economic success. Instead, having passed 'the Knowledge', that amazing feat of learning all the streets of London which licensed black-cab drivers must master, he followed his father by becoming an overeducated cabbie. Eventually, having dropped the foreign Mironov for the more acceptable though falsely Scottish Mirren, he became a low-level civil servant, a driving examiner, in fact. It wasn't long, however, before he rose to a bureaucratic post in the Ministry of Transport.

He never felt at ease with groups of people. He found it hard to go into a pub, or a party. We very rarely had anyone over. Occasionally he, or more probably my mother, felt it was necessary to entertain guests, and then my father would squirm in embarrassment, unable to make the necessary small talk. He was happiest at home, with his children, and later alone on his little old clinker-built boat, the *Curlew*, sailing the muddy waters of the Thames estuary. Though he belonged to the local sailing club, he really only used it for the facilities it afforded him to set off. I don't think he could stand the small-minded snobberies and pretensions.

Incidentally, it was on the *Curlew* that my mild-mannered and kindly father mysteriously turned into a dictatorial gorgon. In the panic of the moment – of which there can be quite a few while sailing – he would snap and shout as we stared bewildered at him. At home, we were the beneficiaries of my father's refusal to be social or ambitious. He had a great and gentle sense of humour; he was always wise and supportive and was adored by all of his children. He was loving, funny and never, as far as I can remember, angry.

Or rather, he did get angry, briefly, but that only came about later, when my sister and I began to see boys. I think he was madly jealous. My father found it very hard to see us grow up like that. But when the time came to go to college, he sent us off with all the love in the world.

He had faults that my mother suffered from. Women were attracted to him and he could be flattered by that; at least that's what my mum said. She was ferociously jealous of him. I think they had a terrific sex life. My mother told me that if they ever had a row, they resolved it in bed. Their rows they kept private, they did not bring their children into it. I think, like me, my father hated confrontation, unless it was political. So I do not remember my parents arguing. Ours was not one of those noisy, passionate Russian households, with rows exploding and disappearing in minutes. Any noise there was came from us three children.

The key to the success of my parents' relationship was the fact that they always found each other interesting and funny. Until their last days together, they talked and laughed together, and held hands and touched. We were a pretty tactile family; we hugged and sat on knees and cuddled until grown up and then some.

Talking was another very important part of my childhood. We had no TV, so we always had dinner together, and talked, usually I seem to remember about philosophical things such as 'Is there such a thing as a soul?' (My parents were both vehement atheists.) Here, my father showed his Russian side, for the Russians love nothing better than a deep philosophical discussion: Do we need art? What is nationhood, and what is nationalism? What is belief? Should tribes intermarry? My father argued that they should, so the whole of humanity would become one race. He hated nationalism, believing it led to conflict. Encouraged by my father, we were gently prodded into thinking for ourselves. It took me years to understand how to make small talk. I couldn't understand conversation that was not about large issues. To this day I am uncomfortable with gossip.

Still cabbying at weekends, my dad would come home from the rank at Sloane Square with gifts for us from the King's Road in Chelsea, which in those days was the hang-out for his kind of people, artists and musicians. My sister and I were the first in school to have coloured tights, much to the approbation of everyone. Me and my friend, Jenny May, insisted on wearing one red stocking and one blue, which must have seemed unbearably challenging to the people of Southend High Street.

Later, my dad was very proud of my achievements as an actress, especially when I was working with the Royal Shakespeare Company. He and my mother used to come up to London on the train and just stand outside the Aldwych Theatre to watch the crowds going in.

Initially, they had both very sensibly been opposed to my ambitions to act. My mother, particularly, having come through the economic deprivations of the Depression and the war, thought it a total waste of an education. However, working with the RSC seemed like a regular job to them. Their fears were economically based, as they rightly surmised that I might not be able to make a living. The regular pay cheque, albeit very small – and of course the nature of the plays (Shakespeare, classy, intellectual) – made them think that maybe I could live as an actress.

So my father lived his quiet and noble life out on the streets of Leigh-on-Sea and on the estuary. This grandson of a Russian countess, who had learned to walk on the family's estate at Kuryanovo, who had survived upheaval and chaos, had created, with my mother, an island of peace and security for his children, and that is why I call it a noble life. After he retired he joined a writing class, got an allotment, and started reading and experimenting with Delia Smith's recipes. He adored Delia, whose column had just begun appearing in the *Evening Standard*. He was happy in his freedom from the routine of work.

And then he died, young really, at the age of sixty-seven, of a very unexpected and I guess massive heart attack. Maybe it was the cream in Delia's recipes.

I was doing a play at the Roundhouse that night, *The Duchess of Malfi*, which is all about death. My mother called me, and I took the call in a corridor twenty minutes before curtain up. My knees crumpled and I found myself on the floor. Then I had a predicament. I knew my understudy was not fully on top of the lines; she had just visited my dressing room and told me, and made me promise never to be off. My mother had said, 'Do the show,' so I did,

Dad on holiday.

but I could not stop crying. One of the speeches in that play is the description of a poor man dying, surrounded only by his loving family. That night I could hardly speak my lines. Immediately after the play ended Liam, my fellow at that time, drove me to Leigh to be with my mother, who was in a complete state of shock.

I never saw my father again. When he died he left neither money nor debts. The sum total of his estate was two hundred and fifty quid.

The funeral took place in a scruffy little crematorium in Westcliff. My brother flew in from Manila. As an atheist, Dad certainly did not believe in the soul or its afterlife. The presiding vicar, who obviously had a drink problem and whom we had never seen before in our lives, tried to say some comforting things about my dad's character and about heaven and so forth, only to be met with the angry, devastated faces of the little group of five – my mother, sister, brother, aunt and myself – huddled together alone in the chapel. Afterwards we went outside. There was no plaque, no headstone.

I looked back and there was the puff of smoke coming from the crematorium that marked my father's existence on this earth. Except, of course, it wasn't. His existence lives forcefully on in the love of his family, and the way we try to live out our lives, inspired by his fun, his decency, his sacrifice, his thoughtfulness.

There was a small postscript to my father's life, one that is very dear to me. Some time after his death I was approached by a woman in a restaurant; I thought it would be for an autograph, or because she had recognised me. She had indeed recognised me but wanted to speak to me as the daughter of my father. She had worked with him, and wanted to ask after him. When I told her that sadly that he had died, she began to tell me of his kindness, cleverness, wit and wisdom. He was, she said, one of the best people she had ever known. She described exactly the person I knew. This encounter was more important to me than any headstone.

This perfectly describes how our father was
with us, loving being a dad. On the opposite
page, Dad doing what he loved, happy at the
helm of a little boat, tootling about.

My cat's name is Flossie.  I call her all sorts
of other things at times, but "Flossie" suits her
soft fluffiness.  You couldn't draw her with clear
lines, her outline is too hazy, like a leafy tree,
but she is full of strong flowing shapes from her
pink ears to her ankle length Victorian drawers.
She is a golden-eyed long haired white Persian Queen.

Flossie is an out-of-work, or rather a retired,
actress who last appeared on TV with Sir Laurence
Olivier in a new Pinter play.  She worked well, but
modestly, and didn't upstage Larry.  The play was a
success and got an EMI award.  But the lights, noise,
bustle and general backstage confusion put a severe
strain on her sense and sensibility.  Sanctuary in
suburbia seemed better for her than occasional
caresses by the famous, and she was fostered by us.

Away from the stage she still has a whiff of
the theatre about her.  She understands ordinary
Green Room talk like "There's my darling pearly
whirly girlie", or "Piss off" and responds correctly,
her timing always absolutely right.  She can show her
feelings in every movement from her head to her
drawers.  But always a Lady - dignified, controlled
and fussy.

Our communication is mostly telepathic.  I can
recognise a range of body signals that give a lot
of information.  She can, for example, say "Thank
you for my dinner" by rubbing her head against my
arm as I put the plate down, or "I don't like your
cooking" by shaking her hind leg at it.  But beyond
that sort of thing something in me can sometimes be
in tune with something in her, the same strings
vibrate, and there is an exchange of sympathy rather
than information.

She has a lovely character, gentle but brave,
loving but independent, since her operation no

35

Dad was always trying different things to satisfy his artistic
side. From music he turned to painting and photography and
then, in retirement, he joined a writing class. He adored our cat
called Flossie; I think they had a psychic connection, which
is strange because Flossie was such a prima donna, but she
undoubtedly returned the passion. Flossie had been hijacked by
my parents from me; they knew my life could not incorporate
the responsibility of a cat. I had fallen in love with her on the
set of 'The Collection' with Laurence Olivier, Malcolm McDowell
and Alan Bates.

longer tortured periodically by the lunacies of sex.
Just a pure heart of gold.

Flossie is also lazy, has fleas, and catches
pigeons. But that is how she was made. She's
unpolluted by knowledge, thank God.

. . . . . . . . . . . . .

This is the Russian side of my father, thoughtful, solitary and deep.

He could also enjoy the absurdity of things like these huge dragons on the set of 'Excalibur'. At his happiest, however, he was surrounded by his closest family. Here he is at one of our many Christmases with his wife, two daughters, his son, his two grandchildren, Basil and Simon, and Mary, Basil's mother.

# Mum

*An extraordinary woman — making her dreams come true*

**Mum was the thirteenth of fourteen children**, born in East London. Her family were trades people in West Ham and Islington; her grandfather had been butcher to Queen Victoria, we were told proudly, and her father had followed him into the business. She grew up on a diet of meat and maybe that was what made her so volatile, and ultimately a vegetarian. You would imagine my Russian father would be the tempestuous temperamental one, but he was calm, thoughtful, and objective. It was my mother who was passionate and unreasonable.

The last five of her huge family were all girls; I have the impression that they were pretty much left to bring each other up, with the older girls caring for and mentoring the younger ones. They remained close all their lives: my auntie Dot, the fourteenth child, used to come to see us every Tuesday, from Barking. Auntie Queen lived in Brighton and ran a bed-and-breakfast hotel (I worked there as a waitress one summer). Auntie Gwen lived in a tiny flat, with no proper bathroom, in Hampstead Road, very poor. She was naturally musical and could play the piano by ear. With two small children, she had been pitilessly abandoned by her husband many years before and left with nothing. He even took the furniture. Husbands could get away with such things in those days before feminism. The sisters had gathered round and helped. Auntie Irene still lived in Ilford, where Mum had grown up, with her family. Then there was Auntie Vera; the beautiful one, who married 'well' in the sense that she married a wealthy industrialist and lived in the Midlands in a big house, with a Roller in the drive. She became an alcoholic. All these sisters were the kindest of aunts and close and supportive of each other, a relationship I now share with my sister.

Perhaps because she had never really experienced mothering from her own mother, it didn't come naturally to Mum. I only found a true and easy relationship with her once the responsibility of being a mother had dropped away from her, after my father died. She was not really cut out for the role, and I don't think she wanted it, although she loved us and my father totally. Some women, more than I think is generally accepted, simply do not feel the call to motherhood. This is not neurosis or some denial of nature, though it must seem incomprehensible to women for whom being a mother is everything. In Mum's day, women were given no real alternative to marriage and motherhood, but it was not something she recommended or advised for her daughters. She was ambitious for us, and like so many of that generation, the key to freedom was education.

My mother was resentful all her life because of her own lack of education. She was self-educated, having left school at fourteen. Though she was very bright and her learning was extensive, with it came a certain hauteur and pretentiousness. In her day, your 'position' in the class system was all-important. I remember her describing the humiliation of having been refused entry to the Army and Navy store in Victoria; it may have been because she didn't have an account there. I think this experience, and many others, informed her passionate determination that my sister and I would have a 'qualification', would go to university and be economically independent women.

Her battle up the social ladder was full of contradiction. It combined a love and respect for the truthfulness, wit and the practicality of the working class, with a desperate need not to be thought of as working class. I think that's why she was so determined to be a stay-at-home mother: she felt it made her middle class. To be a working mother was, to her, to be working class.

We lived in a rather strange, contradictory world. Low income, working class, with my mother often having to scrape at the end of the week to buy food. But with a kind of bohemian, middle-class aspect mixed in.

Mum was a late-night person, often doing the hoovering at one in the morning, and completely unable to get up before ten a.m. As we grew up, we realised we had to get our own breakfast and iron our own uniforms, with the result that we were always scruffy

Mum on the set of *Excalibur*.

and crumpled at school. She was not great at housework. There were always little piles of dust where she had got so far and then been distracted. I think she found it unbearably boring. As soon as my sister and I were old enough, we were recruited to help, which we did with no good grace whatsoever. Every night, however, she cooked a dinner for us to talk over so that when we came home from school, there was a hot and healthy meal on the table.

My mother knew about healthy food, probably from the lessons of the war years. We had home-made wholewheat bread, we were the first in Britain to eat natural yoghurt, and wheat-germ was put on everything. Our meals always included fresh vegetables, and our cakes were home-made. She made spaghetti Bolognese, borscht and curry – exotic dishes for that time. Mum was in fact a vegetarian, those years as a butcher's daughter having given her a horror of dead animals. She never tried to force vegetarianism on us though. If we ate meat infrequently, it was for reasons of economy as much as anything.

My mother loved cats, dogs and birds, and gardens. She kept cats all her life, and always fed the birds; a slight contradiction there as she was always having to save the birds from the cat. She had a spiritual connection with birds in particular. Often, there would be birds' feathers tucked behind mirrors or the teapot in her house. If she found a feather in her path she felt it was a message from the world of birds. She certainly had a relationship with a female blackbird in particular, who brought her chicks to meet her.

Likewise with children. The local kids down the street would come to visit and chat, especially as she grew older. This was not because she was motherly (she wasn't), but because she was genuinely interested in what they had to say. By nature my mother was chatty and gregarious, and suffered as a result of my father's tendency to be a loner.

Another memory that seems to explain her contradictory, dramatic, yearning nature was coming home one day from school and finding the house in chaos, my mother stumbling around with a scarf tied over her eyes. She had read about a blind person, empathised, and wanted to feel what that was like. Method acting really. She had been like that for the last few hours.

Once, when she suspected my father of an affair, she ripped every photo of herself out of all our family albums, so now I only have pictures of her young or old, none from home as we grew up. She often had no control over her tongue or her passions.

She was better with money than my father, who with his socialist leanings saw any kind of wealth or investment as an embarrassment and a class betrayal. When he died he left neither money nor debts. The sum total of his estate was two hundred and fifty quid. My mother, on the other hand, managed on her very meagre budget to squirrel away some money and even eventually bought a few stocks and shares.

Along with many of my generation, I was brought up with a fear and horror of debt. My parents had no money, but neither did they ever owe money to anyone. The mantra was always 'get a roof over your head that no one can take away and you'll be OK'. I have adhered to this mantra.

All our clothes, except school uniforms and cast-offs, were made by Mum. Everything from bikinis to dolls dresses, to tailored jackets and shirts for my dad. My mother and her sisters had grown up making clothes for themselves, and she taught me how to put in a sleeve and how to do a placket. I can see her now, swearing over putting in a zip or aligning a buttonhole. She was a good dress-maker, but these clothes always came out looking a bit home-made, and the only cloth she could afford was the stuff from the reduced-price bin. She had an immense love of fabrics, which I have inherited, and she and I could spend hours in a fabric store feeling the fabrics and dreaming.

Occasionally my parents would collaborate on projects such as tailor-made jackets, with my dad doing the hand-stitching – possibly something he'd learned during his East End days, for that part of London was the domain of the great Jewish tailors – and, memorably, sails in heavy red canvas for the *Curlew*. They couldn't afford to buy sails, so our tiny living room was filled with yards and yards of this thick fabric for weeks and there was an awful lot of swearing. The sails got made and my dad realised his dream of pottering about in a boat, on his own.

I've still got Mum's old treadle Singer sewing machine. She treated it like a beloved relative, oiling it and cleaning it and cosseting it, so it still works beautifully. Sometimes, when I get the urge, I'll spend hours cursing as I put in a sleeve back to front.

In her poverty my mother loved glamour. I am sure she had a touch of the Romany in her. Certainly her father was a horse trader as well as a butcher, and she loved swirly skirts and sparkle. She also loved expensive perfume. My greatest sin as a child was to discover and spill an ancient bottle of perfume she'd had hoarded away for years. A bottle of perfume was the gift my sister and I always brought home for her.

Later in life, she became a regular at the local bridge club, where she was known as Diamond Lil. The diamond rings she had carefully, painfully saved up for over many years, and then haggled over in local second-hand jewellers, would be worn all at the same time. By that time I was able to give her the opportunity to play at the rich life. After Dad died I would always take her on location with me, especially on press junkets, where you are treated as a strange cross between a queen and a slave. Mum got to enjoy the queen side while I performed the slave side. The epitome of this was a trip to Paris, staying at the Hotel Crillon on Place de la Concorde, in a suite the size of her whole house, with a car and a driver at her disposal. The working-class girl from West Ham took to it as if she'd been living in style all her life.

Mum always had an appreciation for what was genuine and spotted affectation a mile off. Whenever she visited me on the set, she would sit in the corner and happily chat to and charm anyone who came by. She chatted as easily with the doorman as the chairman, so in that sense she behaved with true class. In another way she was a complete snob, wanting us to grow up without the estuary accent that now even posh boys at Eton try desperately to emulate. Like my father, she wanted to instil into us children a sense of a wider horizon than the one given to us by the Thames Estuary.

She could be dangerous in her moods, overprotective and jealous, with a tongue capable of cruelty. This probably came from frustration with her position and fear of us falling into a cosy, limited suburban life. Suitors for my sister or myself were not welcomed by either parent, but I think for different reasons. My father did not want to share us, and my mother was terrified that we would succumb to romance, get married and close our lives down too early. She would find truly nasty things to say about anyone we had the temerity to bring home. This resulted in all three of us living secret lives in terms of dating, lives we did not feel we could share with our parents.

In my case, she was totally successful, for, ahead of my generation by about thirty years, I never had any inclination to marry. I couldn't bear the thought. It seemed to me like voluntary imprisonment.

Another subject upon which my mother unleashed her tongue was when I foolishly suggested the possibility of becoming an actress. This was treated with utter disdain and horror. I was called an idiot, a silly little fantasist. After all her good efforts to drag us into that golden world of doctors and lawyers and teachers, it must have seemed like a ridiculously retrogressive idea. She, like my father, wanted me go into law, become a solicitor or a barrister. I remember my dad trying to persuade me that I could use my propensity for drama in the courtroom. But I was too lazy at school for that ever to be a possibility. Here my mother's cruel tongue had no effect, the dream persisted.

In later years, of course, she loved it and all it brought. My parents proved to be the rather cool people they had always been, changing as the society and culture changed.

My mother missed this moment, but in a way I did it for her.

They had to put up with quite a lot from my corner, especially as I became someone occasionally mentioned in the prurient and sex-obsessed press. This all had to be explained away to the bridge players and sailing club members, and still they valiantly supported me. Their bohemian roots came through, and they never blinked.

I wish my parents had been around to see me become a Dame. This might not have been a pure moment of pleasure and pride for them as some of those old left-wing theories of social equality would have lingered on. Nonetheless, in terms of professional success and the triumph of a small family coming really from nowhere and gaining recognition in a country, adopted in one sense, and excluded in another, the moment would have been sweet for both my parents.

Mum would have just loved dressing up and going to the Palace. Once there, they would both have appreciated the actual social equality of the whole thing. Honours went to people from every walk of life; a fine parade of about two hundred ethnically and economically diverse individuals who had all made a contribution. Prince Charles, flanked by two Gurkhas, did the honours with grace, and treated these good people equally and with warmth. Their families, all dressed to the nines, looked on with pride, as did mine, as a military band played showtunes. The whole thing was quite extraordinary and rather moving.

So Mum died without experiencing that, but knowing that at least, thanks to her drive, her dreams and her tongue, her daughters were economically secure, owning their own houses. She had travelled and seen things she could never have imagined, growing up in Ilford, or even in those early days of struggle in Westcliff-on-Sea. She had saved up a little nest egg and paid off her mortgage. She told me that, having loved her life and enjoyed every minute, she was ready to leave it. There was no religion in this. She certainly did not believe in the afterlife; in fact one of the last things she said to me was 'For God's sake, don't get religion!' – failing to see the fundamental contradiction in that request. She was perfectly happy with the thought of oblivion. Many years before, she had donated her body to science, done all the paperwork, so her body was collected before the night was out. There was no funeral, just a tea at the Ritz with her best friends and her little family, which would have been her style, then a year later a wonderful ceremony at Southwark Cathedral. Like my father, she has no headstone, no plaque. My mother lives on for me in my memory and my being.

Here is the young woman my father fell madly and
lustfully in love with.

My mother grew up with many sisters around her, looking after her and mothering her. Here she is as a baby with the closest to her, Gwen and Queenie, and her younger sister Doris. She stayed close to these sisters all her life. I have inherited this from her. My sister and I are very close.

My father with his mother and wife-to-be. His mother and wife share a similarity in the leg department, which I have also inherited. I call them my 'Rooneys.'

Left: Kit, as she was known, at school, hanging out with her girlfriends on the netball team.

Kit was curious about everything and everyone, able to
mix with and chat to LA
cops as well as body builders.
I had a friend in the
competition and took her
along. She was fascinated.
The picture above is of my
mother on the set of 'Blood In, Blood Out', a film Taylor
did about the Latino Mafia in East LA. The reason the
cops were there was because there had been a drive-by
shooting not long before and the caterer had been injured.
I didn't tell Mum.

Kit shows her love
for birds and dogs
(and horses and cats
and all animals).

She loved to visit
LA. Alex and Rio,
Taylor's sons, became
her borrowed grand-
children, and Ghost,
Jasmine and Vato,
her borrowed dogs.
She loved them all.

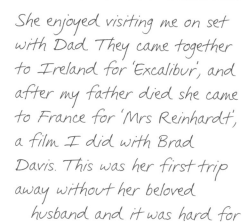

She enjoyed visiting me on set with Dad. They came together to Ireland for 'Excalibur', and after my father died she came to France for 'Mrs Reinhardt', a film I did with Brad Davis. This was her first trip away without her beloved husband and it was hard for her. I was so happy she had the will and the courage to do it. It paved the way for many more years of us sharing things together.

Below: My mother (and some of my father) in my back garden in Fulham, both blissfully unaware of the plant behind them, as they watch my sister barbecue.

Kit in a typical outfit. In my family you dress up for Christmas.

One of my great pleasures was to be able to share my occasional trips to very posh hotels with my mother. Here she is at the Hotel Crillon in Paris, where our suite was the size of her house in Leigh-on-Sea. She took to it like a duck to water. You would have thought she'd done it all her life.

The Committee of Licensed Teachers of
Anatomy of the London Medical Schools

## A SERVICE
## OF THANKSGIVING

for those who have donated their bodies for
Medical Education and Research

at Southwark Cathedral, London Bridge

on Friday 16 May 1997
at 2.30 p.m.

Ginette Molesworth Kitson
Vera Ella Margaret Lane
Leonard Albert Lane
Edmund Bodell Latcham
Diana Philippa Lee
John Albert Lee
Kaye Vera Lloyd
Isabella Edith Stanley Lyall
James Urquhart Mackerrall
Violet Caroline Marchant
Alan Markham
Gertrude Marson
Edward Charles Mason
Freda Matthews
Janet Barrowman McLeod
Lilian Mary McKenzie
Marjorie Lindsell Meek
Joan Emerton Melville
Ronald Mercer
Ernest George Middleton
John Miller
Edith Mary Mills
Kathleen Alexandra Ena Matilda Mirren
Arnold Keith Moon
Gordon Evelyn Michael Moore
Hilda Gwendoline Morris
Roy Moss
Margaret Winifred Moylan
Dennis Michael Mullan
Winifred Mary Mussell
Gladys Alice Mytton
Doris Hilda Eliza Nicholls
Mary Doreen O'Reilly
Percy Noel Oldreive
Edward Clifford Lewis Ovenden
Dorothy Frances Packham
Leonard James Palmer
Robina Parker
Arthur Edward Parker
Robert Patrick Simeon Pattenden
Thomas Charles Perry
Archibald William Henry Pettifer
Anne Philipp
Lucy Elizabeth Phillpott

- 17 -

When my mother died, she left her body to science; this was a typical gesture on her part, a dramatic, idiosyncratic, self-effacing, attention-seeking gesture, deeply felt nonetheless and useful. I was with her, the night she died. We knew she had not long to live. That afternoon I had carefully painted her fingernails a bright, life-affirming red. I wanted those young medical students soon to take her body apart to know that this was a woman who was and had loved. She died at about three in the morning. I kissed her goodbye, although she had already gone, and took her wedding ring off her finger. I still regret not cutting off her long and beautiful hair to keep, never cut or coloured or permed. She would have loved the theatricality of the service of thanksgiving, held by the London Medical Schools in Southwark Cathedral about a year later. It was non-denominational, non-religious, with a glorious choir, and the servers were all young medical students. She would have loved it, as my sister and I did. She would have loved the idea of being surrounded by young people, eager to learn and to explore; she would have loved the fact that instead of a homely funeral celebration, her small group of mourners went to the Ritz for tea. She would have loved also the fact that she had the longest name in the list of donors: Kathleen Alexandra Ena Matilda.

# Childhood

*Growing up with my brother and sister*

**I was born in Queen Charlotte's Hospital**, Chiswick, the fastest birth on record at that time. I wonder if anyone has broken it yet? I was two weeks late, but then came into the world in a big rush at about two in the morning. In fact I was born in the corridor, as the nurses did not believe my mother when she said she was giving birth there and then. It had only been twenty minutes since she went into labour. Ever since I have always done things quickly at the last minute, procrastinate then panic and get the job done quick.

I missed the end of the Second World War by two months, but the shadow of that terrible time hung over the first part of my life. My parents had spent the majority of the war in London. My mother was evacuated to the Forest of Dean, a place where I was later to find great happiness, but I don't think she could live without my father, who was driving an ambulance in the East End. So my parents lived through the Blitz. My mother told me of walking down a street where a jeweller's and a pet shop had been hit the night before, and seeing watches and necklaces on the pavement, and birds fluttering about. She said there was very little looting by ordinary people in London. However, there was certainly a black market, with goods available for those with enough money to pay for them, and I think this fuelled my parents' hatred of a class and economic system that excluded so many.

The first house I remember living in was in Westcliff-on-Sea. My family moved there after the birth of my younger brother, when I was about two or three years old. At that time, long before Ryanair, EasyJet and the rise of the Spanish holiday resorts, Southend's coastline was the holiday playground for the working men and women of the East End. With its mud flats, its 'Longest Pier in the World', its fish-and-chip shops. candyfloss, funfairs and, of course, its pubs, Southend was the ideal place to escape the bombed-out ruins of London. The general idea seemed to be to take the train from Fenchurch Street, or Dagenham, or Barking, sit on the beach come rain or shine, go to the pub, have a fight, throw up and go home again very satisfied.

To my parents it seemed an ideal place to bring up a family on very little money, because of course, it was a whole lot of other things too. It has a very special beauty, best described by Joseph Conrad in the pre-story to *Heart of Darkness*. The ship is hauled to, waiting for the tide as the story within a story is told, and Conrad perfectly describes the strange colourful beauty of those mud flats, the wideness of the sky, and the magic of that ancient river with its ferocious tides. Those eddies and channels of water as the Thames rushes in over the mud has claimed many victims who failed to see the danger until it was too late.

I loved the look of Southend. It gave me a taste for out-of-season holiday places that has never left me. The shuttered ice cream parlour, the desolate slot machines, the coloured lights swaying in the cold wind. It also gave me a taste for the fairground, for the carnival, although maybe that's my mother's Romany side coming through.

East Essex was a bit like the North of England, always about eight years out of date, but at the same time on the cutting edge for certain fashions. Mods came originally from Basildon, just down the road, and men from the East End have traditionally had a sense of fashion, loving good tailoring and a sharp suit. Also many bands and music trends have come from those grey streets of the estuary hinterland.

In the early days in Westcliff, we children lived out on the street with the neighbours' kids, safe from cars for there were none to speak of, and no other predators to fear, it seemed. I was quite happy with this little band of friends, but the primary school filled me with terror. Not the classroom, but the horrible playground, with its cold and stinky outside lavatories where the doors did not lock or even close, and its insane childish cruelties, its bullying, and its incomprehensible rules of social engagement.

It was in the playground of Hamlet Court primary school that I committed one of the most horrible, shameful acts of my life. I must have been about seven at the time. There was a girl in my class called Geraldine and I really liked her; she was one of my few friends, maybe my only friend. She was smart, bright and fun. Then one day I told her I couldn't play with her any more because she was Jewish. Some foul little edict had come down from the 'popular' kids, the bullies

The three young Mironovs.

and dictators who declared public policy. Wimp that I was, cowardly and weak jerk, I obeyed the playground Nazis instead of following my true feelings. I have never forgotten the look on her face, standing there in the bike shed. She sensibly never spoke to me again, and I have felt deeply guilty ever since. That was the world of the playground as I remember it. Small wonder that the sound of the bell going off for break would fill me with dread.

Well, there was a brief period when I did enjoy playtime. That was when 'beads' became the rage, with all the children under the age of nine bartering little bits of coloured glass. In no time, like the Tulip Bubble in Holland, trading beads became a mad obsession for everyone, including the horrible boys. It was a mini Wall Street bonanza bull market as these baubles, nicked or begged from Mum, exchanged hands many times over in one fifteen-minute break, moving from one cotton wool-lined matchbox to another. I quickly grasped the importance of presentation and salesmanship, and bartered one broken bead into a whole collection. But, just like the Dutch tulips, 'beads' waned in popularity, and we were left with the usual activities of bullying, betraying, teasing, fighting and general loneliness.

My other great horror at that time was attending children's birthday parties. These were just like the nightmare of playtime, only organised by grown-ups who seemed to delight in inventing ghastly competitive games that always left me feeling hopeless, inadequate and sometimes sick. One, I remember, involved being blindfolded and made to put your hand into a nasty-feeling wet mixture, which we were told was vomit. You had to rummage around looking for a present. Disgusting.

My first performance, as I recall, was as the Virgin Mary. I was about six years old. I had no lines but I did have a gorgeous blue veil with stars all over it. I remember that veil so well. It gave me an everlasting love of costume. All I had to do was sit there. The perfect role! I wish they had all been that easy. Sit tight, don't move, say nothing and let the costume do all the work.

My next role introduced me to the ever present and inevitable unfairness of my eventually chosen profession, especially the casting process. By this time I was about eight. My class had been told to line up and walk in an orderly manner to the hall. As usual, I was one of the last to get into line. When we got to the hall it transpired that this was the casting call for the production of

*Four and Twenty Blackbirds* that was to be our class's contribution to the school's end-of-year show. The teacher started at the beginning of the line: 'You will be the king, you the queen, you the princess, you the cook, you the prince, you the chamberlain ...' and, pointing at the rest of the line, 'all the rest of you the blackbirds!'

Weeks later, hunched under the pie crust with twenty-three other eight-year-olds in ill-fitting black leotards, inhaling that distinctive odour of smelly plimsolls, waiting our cue to pop out and hearing the princess, wearing pink and gold and wearing a crown say her words badly ... well, my resentment knew no bounds. However, it was good early training for a career where I would often lose a part to a prettier person, or to someone who was at the front of the line while I was at the back.

My parting performance at Hamlet Court primary was the lead role in *Hansel and Gretel*. You would think I'd have been grateful, but I wasn't. I was terrified, because the lines all came in a book, a slim, red, cloth-bound book that I remember to this day. I could not imagine that it was possible to learn that many lines. I begged my mother to get me out of it. She wisely refused. To this day when I look at a play my heart sinks, as I cannot believe I will be able to learn all those lines.

In fact I was never the kind of little girl who naturally loves to perform, or rather be looked at. Embarrassment came easily to me and acting, even in my schooldays, was more to do with disappearing than 'look at me'. Even now, my relationship with the audience is ambivalent. I am vaguely embarrassed by the idea of being looked at, have to put it out of my mind and get swept away by the imaginative world the audience is allowing me to engage with.

At home, away from these traumas, life was poor but sweet. We also had no central heating, of course, and our house was freezing cold in the winter. I remember ice on the inside of the windows in our bedrooms and the tiny bathroom. My mother would struggle every morning trying to light the voracious coal-fired boiler that supplied our hot water, and then the coal fire that was our only source of heat. It was there I learned to light a fire – a useful skill – with the help of nuggets of paper and then more paper held over the front of the fireplace.

When I was younger we had no washing machine, no car, and no refrigerator. The butter would sit in a bowl of water and the meat in a 'meat-safe' – a mesh cover that kept the flies off. I can't remember when we got a fridge for the first time but it must have been a momentous day for my mother. We had no television in my house, until after I left home for college, and no radio to speak of. We did have an enormous thing called a 'radiogram' that was the size of a coffin and seemed to take up most of the living room yet serve no purpose; the radio bit hardly worked and we only had about three records to play on it, one being *Peter and the Wolf*, which I can still sing bits of. My mother was a total musical snob, although unmusical herself, and we were only allowed to listen to classical music, which meant that when I first heard Elvis I almost fainted.

My Russian grandfather came to live with us, and we also had Brutus the dog, who'd originally belonged to my flighty Auntie Olga, and a sweet cat called Tiddles.

Aunt Olga was my father's younger sister, born in Britain and very beautiful, in an earthy Russian way. She had been a chorus girl in London, working at the Windmill briefly, before marrying first a successful car salesman and then the successful East End villain George Dawson.

From her first marriage she had a daughter, my impossibly beautiful and kind cousin Tania, who became a supermodel in the early sixties, just before the rise of Twiggy. Tania and Olga, along with my Russian grandmother (who by then had long since left my grandfather), lived a very glamorous life in comparison to ours. They sailed in yachts off the South of France with Uncle George, sweeping into our life from time to time bearing gifts of cast-off clothing, items which were always expensive and lovely. I think Olga must have given my mother the bottle of French perfume that sat in the bottom of her wardrobe for many years, losing its smell, but treasured nonetheless.

My first leading role, as Gretel.

After distributing their gifts, Olga, Granny and Tania would head off again, leaving a whiff of perfume and corruption. George eventually did time for his misdeeds – fraud, mostly – serving about three years of a six-year sentence. I believe he was instrumental in the escape of one of the Great Train Robbers from prison. He was shocked by and disapproved of the rise of the violent London villains like the Kray twins. To him, villainy was all about the con, and using your brain rather than force. He was incapable of doing anything straight, even paying the butcher's bill.

Cousin Tania survived this extraordinary upbringing and came out miraculously a loyal and generous person, educating her brothers with her earnings as a young model and always supporting her mother. Even so, Olga and Granny finished up in a council flat on the top floor of a high-rise block in Southend. Despite having lived all their lives in expensive hotels and glamorous rented apartments, they were perfectly happy there. It was the first place they could call home. Granny became very enamoured of the local Labour Party and council that had given her security at last. She went canvassing for them, which, as her English was very bad, and spoken with a very strong Russian accent, must have been disconcerting for the people she door-stepped in those Cold War days.

My sister, Katherine, known now as Kate, is a couple of years older than me and my brother, Peter, was three years younger. Peter was in fact christened Peter Basil, like his grandfather and great-great-grandfather, following on the Russian family tradition.

My sister was and is for ever my Big Sister to whom I will always defer. She is my best friend. She was the one I shared my first bedroom with. One night, she recalls me, still asleep, getting into her bed on top of her, and continuing to sleep uninterrupted. She was the one who first had to walk me to primary school; a walk that must have taken about half an hour. She was the big girl at St Bernard's Convent, smoothing my path there. And she was the one who had to fight all the first teenage battles with my parents, once again making my passage easier when my turn came.

Growing up in a small house with no money or resources led to many conflicts between my sister and myself, almost always due to my appropriation of articles belonging to her: hair slides, skirts, pencils. We had to fight for our space, and all three of us did. It's strange, but while living in the closest of physical circumstances, we nonetheless led completely different lives. Kate loved sailing and went off crewing in races on little sailing dinghies while I hung around art galleries. It was only after we left the circumscribed environment of the house in Leigh that we could see and love each other fully.

My sister was the first to leave home, going off to London, the big city that was always singing its siren song for us from the other side of Dagenham. She got a place at a teachers' training college, with rooms in Kensington. She was studying Home Economics, as it's now known, and college launched her on a long, happy and successful career as a teacher. Two years later, I got into college (again, a teachers' training school, where I studied Speech and Drama). I went to visit her and had the most extraordinary experience of falling in love with my own sister. In this new environment, I saw her clearly for the first time and loved what I saw, and ever since we have been very close. I've never had children, so my sister has generously shared her family with me, and now Kate, her son Simon and his three children form the centre of my life together with my husband and his two sons.

I loved my little brother Peter in spite of the fact that he was – or so it seemed to Kate and me – impossibly spoilt. For all my mother's natural feminism, she couldn't or wouldn't accept the concept of boys doing housework, whereas it was required of us girls. I remember her trying to teach me how to iron a man's shirt, which I resisted. Peter was also given a tiny boat, left by an uncle who died. In fact it went to the right person, because Peter became a very good sailor and won many races on the Thames. He sailed all of his adventuresome life. My brother was simply one of the most extraordinary people I have ever known, though as in the case of my sister, I didn't really know him at home.

I remember that nasty moment when I realised he was bigger than me, and therefore no longer under my command. Just on the verge of banging his head against the wall, I suddenly noticed I was looking up at him. Quick change of plan! As I became a teenager, he turned into an impenetrable spotty, gangly pubescent, interested in bombs, boats and boy things. He was always out and about, and was the only one of us not intimidated by my mother's caustic tongue. I remember some spectacular rows and banging doors that Kate and I could aspire to but never dare to emulate.

Having failed the Eleven-plus exam, Peter was destined for the kind of secondary school education that was more to do with carpentry than Latin. This was not necessarily a bad thing for him, for he was always practical, a man of action, not destined to become an intellectual, but he was nevertheless very clever. He went on to lead an extraordinary life of adventure working as an engineer, and later a trained commercial plane pilot. He also turned out to be an incredible storyteller. He had the potential to be a much better writer than Kate and myself, for all our studying of Shakespeare and Thomas Hardy. Sadly, the only writing he did was in letters home. He could make you cry with laughter at his stories of misadventure in exotic places.

For all his talent, the school he went to did not have the resources to teach someone like him, so he left when he was fifteen. At the age of sixteen he got a local girl pregnant. Back then, it was the all-time sin to either get pregnant or get someone else pregnant out of wedlock. Of course there was no birth control, or even sex education in schools. The girl was sent to one of those homes for unmarried pregnant girls run by well-meaning but rigid people. I visited her there. She was a lovely girl, smart and sensitive, and did not deserve this fate. Her child, a girl, was adopted. I often think of that niece of mine.

Not long afterwards my brother joined the army. I think my parents felt he was in danger of running completely wild, so he was encouraged to make this step, and to take a course in soil analysis while there. After about two years in the army he realised it was not for him and tried to leave, whereupon the army made it very difficult for him to get out. My parents fought for his right to leave, and they became part of a movement to change the law, stopping very young men from signing away their lives to the armed forces. This lobbying proved successful and the law was subsequently changed.

So Peter got out of the army and began a life of travel and amazing adventure. He went off to Africa – the Kalahari Desert, South Africa, New Guinea and Libya – building roads through some of the most inaccessible terrain in the world, in the kind of places where you have to hunt, kill and cook the food for the workforce each night. He worked with many different races in his time, but like Rider Haggard, his favourite people were the Zulu. He had many wonderful tales about them. He told me that the Zulu do not name a baby until its character has appeared, and ignore the given name of the people with whom they come in contact, preferring to find an appropriately descriptive name. Their name for him translated as 'Where is he?'. It was a perfect name for him. He was never to be found where you expected.

Incredibly brave, somewhat foolhardy, 'Where is he?' often sailed, or flew, into dangerous waters. Having gained his private plane licence, he went on

Kate and me, ready for school.
Overleaf: The cast of *Hansel and Gretel*.

to qualify for a commercial pilot's licence, which allowed him to indulge his love of flying. And on his travels he managed to get himself caught up in coups and all sorts of scraps. Funny and self-deprecating, opinionated and prejudiced, even though he wasn't a drinker he loved to hang out in some of the dodgiest bars in the world, with some of the dodgiest men. Peter grabbed life by the balls. He was absolutely not destined for suburbia.

Maybe he inherited his father's love of solitude. He didn't need or want a family, and was not a good father to the only child he had (or, at least, the only officially acknowledged child), my lovely nephew Basil. Eventually he found the Philippines, fell in love with that country, and stopped travelling. It was there that he died, aged fifty-four, refusing to return to Britain for treatment.

I visited him there, eight years before he died, on my way back from the Tokyo Film Festival with Taylor. I found him obsessed with making the perfect bra for the many girlfriends he had, who worked in the various bars in the area. At that time the only bras available in the markets were sad, heavy, overstructured things. He spent hours hunched over a sewing machine, just like my parents making their sails, working out how to get various bits of nylon lace to fit together. Like Howard Hughes, he approached the job from an engineer's point of view. He was also outraged because the Philippine government in Manila was closing down those girlie bars in the hope of regenerating the area. The girls in the bars and their mamasans had become his family. He could not deal with independent and successful women like his sisters. He was somewhat retrogressive in many of his attitudes.

Although I had not seen him since my father died about ten years previously, it was clear he did not really want me there. He arranged for us to stay in a hotel, far from his apartment, and on the first night suggested to Taylor that he should leave me in the hotel while the two of them headed off to some bars to pick up girls. He was taken aback when Taylor said he did not think that was a good idea.

Luckily, two things then happened. Taylor had to fly back to Tokyo to pick up an award he had won at the festival, and no sooner had he gone than a hurricane blew in and I was stuck; the airport was closed. I checked out of the hotel and presented myself at Peter's doorstep. He had to take me in. I spent the next four days with him, loving him as much as ever and showing him I was still his family, and his big sister to boot.

That was the last time I saw him, and I am very grateful that I had at least that time with him.

My friend Geraldine and the look on her face when
I betrayed her. It was an image that haunted me,
and many years later I did this painting to try to
confront my guilt.

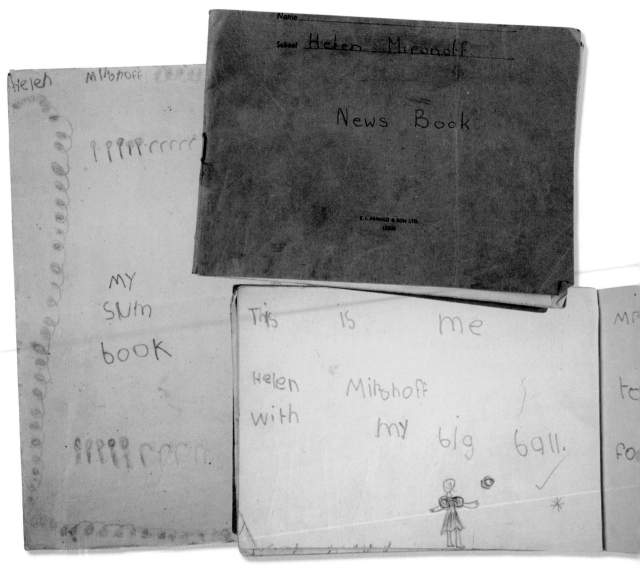

My
sum
book

News Book

E. J. ARNOLD & SON LTD.
LEEDS

This        is        me

Helen        Mironoff
with                my        big        ball.

R.B.1
16
MINISTRY OF
FOOD
1953-1954
SERIAL NO.
AN 139994
1

**RATION BOOK**

Surname MIRREN        Initials Helen L
Address

IF FOUND
RETURN TO
ANY FOOD
OFFICE

F.O. CODE No.
E.J/1

I was never very good
at school. Little did I
know that my sum book
was only the beginning of
years of struggle.

I grew up as a young
child in the post-war years
under the restrictions of
rationing. Probably just
as well, as sweets were
practically non-existent.

Here are a group of pictures from my childhood.
A portrait by a professional, holding a borrowed toy, but
posing nonetheless. A birthday party. I hated all birthday
parties except the ones my parents gave. They were fun.
Here we are with the neighbours that we played in the street
with, and our cousin Tania, destined to be a top model.

Above: At this age I loved ballet, took lessons and even practised on my own. This picture was taken before going off to take a dancing exam. I was never that neat otherwise.
Top right: Me aged twelve.

Left: The house
I spent my early years
in, in Satanita Road.
Below: This picture,
found in Moscow, shows
my grandfather walking
with my brother and
Tiddles and Brutus –
a family outing.

Our terrible slobbery
dog, Brutus, that had
been foisted on us by
Auntie Olga. He loved
the cat Tiddles. They
would go for walks
together, and Brutus
looked after Tiddles'
kittens. They would sleep
curled up between his legs and
he carefully guarded them.

These pictures
of my brother
doing boy stuff
caused much
merriment. They
encapsulate
masculinity
to me.

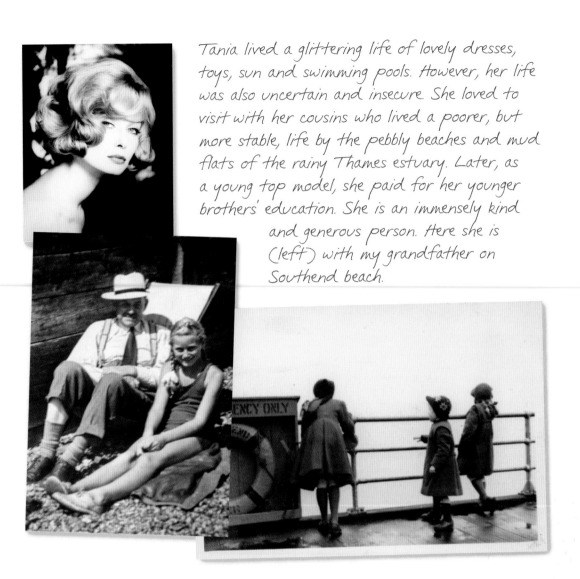

Tania lived a glittering life of lovely dresses, toys, sun and swimming pools. However, her life was also uncertain and insecure. She loved to visit with her cousins who lived a poorer, but more stable, life by the pebbly beaches and mud flats of the rainy Thames estuary. Later, as a young top model, she paid for her younger brothers' education. She is an immensely kind and generous person. Here she is (left) with my grandfather on Southend beach.

Right: Dressed up to go out. We had few clothes apart from our uniforms.

The picture on the left is the last one of us all together before we went our separate ways, Kate and I to college and Peter into the army. The one above is the very last picture of the three of us together. Peter had come back from the Philippines for a brief visit.

# Southend

*Becoming an Essex Girl*

**After primary school** I followed my sister's example and passed that terrible and divisive exam called the Eleven-plus and thanks probably to the efforts of my parents, entered St Bernard's Convent Grammar School. Being a parochial Roman Catholic school, it was thought of as one of the best in the neighbourhood. I don't know how much soul-searching, or rather morality-searching, my atheist parents had to go through before reaching the conclusion that this was where they wanted their daughters to attend.

St Bernard's was a convent for Bernardine nuns, who wore the full black robes with a white wimple. It was an enclosed order. The nuns' lives were completely circumscribed by the school's cramped grounds. To enter the school was to smell lavender polish and a faint whiff of incense. The halls were always immaculately polished, crucifixes and statues of the Virgin Mary placed all about. The only form of exercise those nuns had was to walk in pairs around and around a very small patch of grass. Years later, I revisited the school. The nuns were long gone, having been moved to another convent, and I was shown the bedrooms where they lived out their lives, behind the mysterious doors we were never allowed to pass through. They were minute cells with tiny windows. My admiration for them grew.

The head of the school went by the impressive name of Dame Mother Mary Mildred. At some point in her life she had received an honour, I don't know what for. She was old and small and as impressive as her name. She had one eye that drooped and a face red with broken veins. She exuded a strict sort of kindness, and a wisdom that was completely innocent of modern life. I remember my first meeting with her so very clearly. She gave me advice that I grew to appreciate more and more as life went on: beware of fear. I think she must have guessed that I was terrified, and would often be so. She tried to make me understand how destructive fear can be. It was advice I frequently thought back on later in life, whenever I found myself in a state of fear. In spite of her inevitably narrow outlook, I always had huge respect for her.

Later, when she learned that I wanted to become an actress, she simply could not understand. To her the only viable ambition in life for a woman was to marry and have children, good Roman Catholics all, or to become a nun. I let her down badly on all counts. I did, however, go through a brief period of wanting to become a nun, seduced by the iconography and romance of the cult of Mary, and the peaceful non-competitive world of the order. To the great alarm of my atheist parents, I started building my version of an altar at home, incorporating candles, draperies, and sparkly things. I suspect it was the incipient drama of the whole thing that appealed to me. To this day I love a good altar, to whatever god or goddess, and I always light a candle. My religious phase did not last long, overtaken by drama of a different sort, and of course, boys.

At St Bernard's I became part of a group of friends, noticeable for our attempts to change or adapt the school's uniform code, which was strictly upheld and went something like this: 1 (Most important and very, very bad to not obey) Always wear your beret (in winter) and straw hat (summer) when going to or from school; 2 Always wear a tie if not in summer uniform; 3 Never open your shirt collar; 4 Never roll or push up your sleeves; 5 Skirts must touch the ground when kneeling; 6 Always wear 'sensible' shoes. Of course we found 101 different ways to flout these rules, and make the uniform our own, mostly related to rolling up our skirts at the waist to make them instant miniskirts that could be let down in a second. I love to see schoolkids in uniform now, boys as well as girls, and spot what changes they have invented. It's amazing what you can do with a tie.

It was around this time that I was first exposed to modern music, through finding the very crackly sounds coming from Radio Luxembourg, though it meant having to lie on the ground with my ear right up alongside the coffin in the living room. I also had the fortune to meet a local luminary who was at art school … so impressive. His name was Vic Stanshall, and he later became a musician and cult figure when he changed his name to Viv and formed the Bonzo Dog Doo Dah Band. Uncle Vic, as we knew him, played Sonny Terry and Brownie McGhee for me … 'You've got bad blood, baby, I think that you need a shot, Let me stick my old needle in you, baby. Mmmmmm, what a lot you got.' I didn't quite grasp what it meant, but it was like an electric shock going through my system. As an unmusical person who cannot sing a note or hold a tune, this is the one song

My best girlfriends at St Bernard's.

I can remember (the Catholic hymns are long gone). I can still hear the needle descending on to the record. To this day, I love the blues. Pop, being so clean and jolly, had nothing on it to my mind, even then. I never became a fan of pop music, never followed any band or pop star. I preferred Edith Piaf, or Big Bill Broonzy. I made an exception with Elvis; I still remember hearing 'Heartbreak Hotel' for the first time – one of the truly great classics. It made my heart stop beating.

I was also a jazz fan of sorts. Not that I was an expert in any way, but I'd go along with my friends to a jazz afternoon that took place in a disused cinema on Sunday afternoons, at a time when one could legitimately sneak off. It was traditional live jazz, and the venue was full of very boring blokes with beards and sandals, but the music was fantastic. We would go there and dance our hearts out, jiving to jazz with each other and spurning the boring blokes. All this would have appalled my mother. Even jazz was unacceptable. None of our entertainment included alcohol, let alone drugs. I didn't like pubs then, and still don't particularly care for them now. I didn't like the kind of men that went to pubs, or the role given to women in them. I didn't like the drink that was served in them and how it was served. Later in life I discovered the American dive and the cocktail and found my place as far as bars and alcohol were concerned.

And all the time I was growing up, there was the heartbeat of the big city, the big smoke, London, echoing down the Thames. We went to London with the school – I'd get there early for once, straight to the back of the bus, wave to blokes in Dagenham out the back window, toilet stop at the public lavs in Gants Hill, then off to the Tate or a museum. These trips were so exciting. It was on one of these excursions that I was taught to do the twist by a black GI in Hyde Park. There was no way in the world I was going to stay in Southend and not try my way in the big city in some way or other.

In the meantime there was the pebbly beach in the (usually wet) summer, and the occasional trip out to the Ray. The Ray is a strip of water that is all that remains of the Thames when the tide goes out. On a hot day the sailing community would sail out with the tide, then picnic out there on the sandy mud while the tide went out, sailing in again with the next tide.

I never got the hang of sailing, except in a very superficial way. All that 'ready about!' and 'lee-ho!' did nothing for me. I once blotted my reputation as a crew member by jumping overboard in a temper right in the middle of a race. My idea of sailing is to sit on the foredeck with an iced drink, floating on a clear, blue, warm and sparkling sea, not tear up and down the dark, muddy estuary in the pouring rain and gusting wind, with blistered fingers from all that tacking and hauling on ropes. My sister took to it, and went on to sail the Atlantic and many other seas. Likewise my brother.

I was a landlubber, preferring to mooch about dreaming that I would be magically discovered and given my big chance on some stage, or become the muse to a famous artist who happened to be passing. I also tried to learn French, deeply impressed by the French boys who would turn up in the summer holidays to improve their English. I scored one as my first proper boyfriend. His name was Jean Louis Alpeyrie, and his parents were Jews from Paris who had miraculously, and with real suffering, survived the terrible danger of the war and Nazi occupation.

One day, I had a bit of luck when a man – an actor from the local theatre, of all people – knocked me down on a Zebra crossing. Talk about fate! He was completely in the wrong, I was slightly injured and I got some money from his insurance for my pains. I used this money for a visit to Paris, flying on my first plane, to visit Jean Louis and his family. For some insane reason to do with national pride in animal culture, I took with me a leg of lamb, uncooked. Jean Louis's mother was polite but bemused. They were very kind to me, and I remember them with great fondness.

Recently I found Jean Louis through Google. When we were teenagers I had shared with him my dream of becoming an actress and he had told me he wanted to become a businessman; and that's exactly what he had done. He's now a successful business headhunter in New York. He was also smart and thoughtful and funny. I admired my own good taste.

Apart from the French boys, I was attracted by the style of the art students and wanted to get to know them. I loved art at school, and when I wasn't imagining myself walking around with a script under my arm, I dreamt of being an artist, walking around with a sketchpad.

The cinema just did not exist for me at that time. I might have gone once or twice with a boy, but I don't remember any of the films I saw. The kind of British or American films that were shown in a small town in Britain at that time were of no interest to me. The first film that made an impression on me was *L'Avventura* by Antonioni, which I stumbled upon in Brighton the year I worked as a waitress for my Auntie Queen. That I remember clearly. I thought Monica Vitti was gorgeous and the story wonderfully mysterious. From that moment on I loved foreign films.

It's hard to deconstruct exactly where that dream of being an actress came from. There were a few markers. The most important, I think, were two very different theatrical performances I attended as a child. Here I must say that my parents could not afford to take us to the theatre or the cinema, we had no TV at home, and my school did not view live performances as a part of the curriculum. My experience of theatre was therefore limited to these two instances.

The first was a show at the end of the pier. A mile and a quarter out in the wet and windy Thames we saw what I guess was a rather sad summer show called *Out of the Blue*. I was six. I absolutely loved it. The comedian, Terry Scott (long before he became a famous TV star), played a naughty little boy, stuffing his overweight form into too-tight short trousers. He made me fall off my seat with laughter, but the best bit for me was the dancing girls who came on and twirled around with bits of blue chiffon. I thought it was the most magical thing I had ever seen. I have never forgotten it.

The next performance was an amateur production of *Hamlet* by the Southend Shakespearean Society. This production took place in our local theatre, the Palace, a beautiful Edwardian theatre of a perfect size. I must have been about thirteen, the best age to experience Shakespeare for the first time. It was in all probability a very bad production, I certainly remember tights that were falling down, but the power of the story and the exoticism of the characters were overwhelming. I don't think I responded so much to the incredible poetry of the play, or the depth of the philosophy, or the understanding of human psychology, but simply to the fact that the world presented was so much more exciting than the rather drab world around me. Ophelia going mad, Gertrude swallowing the poison, Hamlet talking to a skull, Hamlet accidentally killing Polonius, Hamlet and Laertes fighting to the death … Life was not like that in Leigh-on-Sea, or at least, not down my road.

That production brought me to Shakespeare. I went home and read the plays, looking again for character rather than poetry. I couldn't understand most of it (I still can't) but the plays rewarded me with a parade of fantastic female characters: Joan of Arc, written as a violent madwoman, the bloody, vengeful Queen Margaret – these were the characters I loved.

At St Bernard's our one concession to the world of drama was the Shakespeare Cup. This little silver cup was presented to the winner of a competition in which each form, from the third year on, had to prepare and perform a scene from Shakespeare, without the help of a teacher and with no set or costumes. That year I took charge. I had read and loved *The Tempest*, attracted by the magic of Ariel and Caliban, so I suggested a scene from that play. No one wanted to play Caliban, which suited me fine, because that was the role I wanted; the pathos and tragedy appealed to me. I don't think we won that year, but we did the next, when I got to do the mad scene of Ophelia from *Hamlet*. I played it again many years later at the RSC, but never so well again.

It was on the basis of this work that my blessed English teacher, Mrs Welding, suggested I apply for the National Youth Theatre. I wonder if I would ever have managed to become an actress if it had not been for Mrs Welding. In the past of many artists, especially ones coming from an unexpected background, you will find a very fine teacher. Mrs Welding was the kind of teacher that made every lesson a pleasure. She was not a noisy, performing kind of teacher, full of charisma and character. She was modest, quiet, and measured, but she had a way of making literature leap to life. Everyone loved her. We who had the privilege of being taught by her immediately improved, and learned to love literature, at least while she was teaching it.

At this point I should also mention Miss Angel. Miss Angel was the most glamorous of all our teachers. I was never quite sure what her function was, other than that it had something to do with elocution. At that time it was simply not acceptable to have any kind of regional accent. I am not just talking about acting, although of course that rule held sway there, too. No, even in the world of work, you had a distinct advantage if you spoke in that BBC accent, and of course it showed that you were a nice young lady. Certainly Miss Angel gave private elocution lessons, and occasionally a class in elocution. Maybe that was why my mother was keen for us to go to St Bernard's.

Miss Angel's other function was to direct the yearly nativity play, St Bernard's official salute to the world of drama. This did not require much invention on her part, as each year, no matter who played each role, the cast had to say exactly the same words, wear exactly the same costumes and make exactly the same moves. For a few years running I played Eve being thrown out of the Garden of Eden – our nativity started right at the beginning, with original sin. Eve was a much better part than Mary, the only other good role being that of the Angel Gabriel, but the head girl or someone very tall and beautiful always played that. Oh, Adam, what shall we do? Whither shall we go? I can't believe I remember the words! Best of all, Eve's costume was fabulous, if deeply incorrect: a mouldy, very old and somewhat smelly piece of real leopardskin, never cleaned, with the sweat of who knows how many former performances soaked into it. It was sexy.

So Miss Angel's contribution was really just to get the costumes out of their boxes, get them ironed, corral us and make sure we did exactly as had been done year after year. Miss Angel was not an icon to us because of her inspiration, but rather because she was simply the most glamorous thing on two very elegant legs. She always wore the sheerest of stockings, her shoes were never scuffed, her feet narrow and elegant. She was very slim, very graceful. She was also very nice. Not strict, not particularly concerned really, but rising above it all and somehow not like a teacher. She was gorgeous, and we loved her. I was happy to hear shortly after I left that she had married and gone to live in Africa.

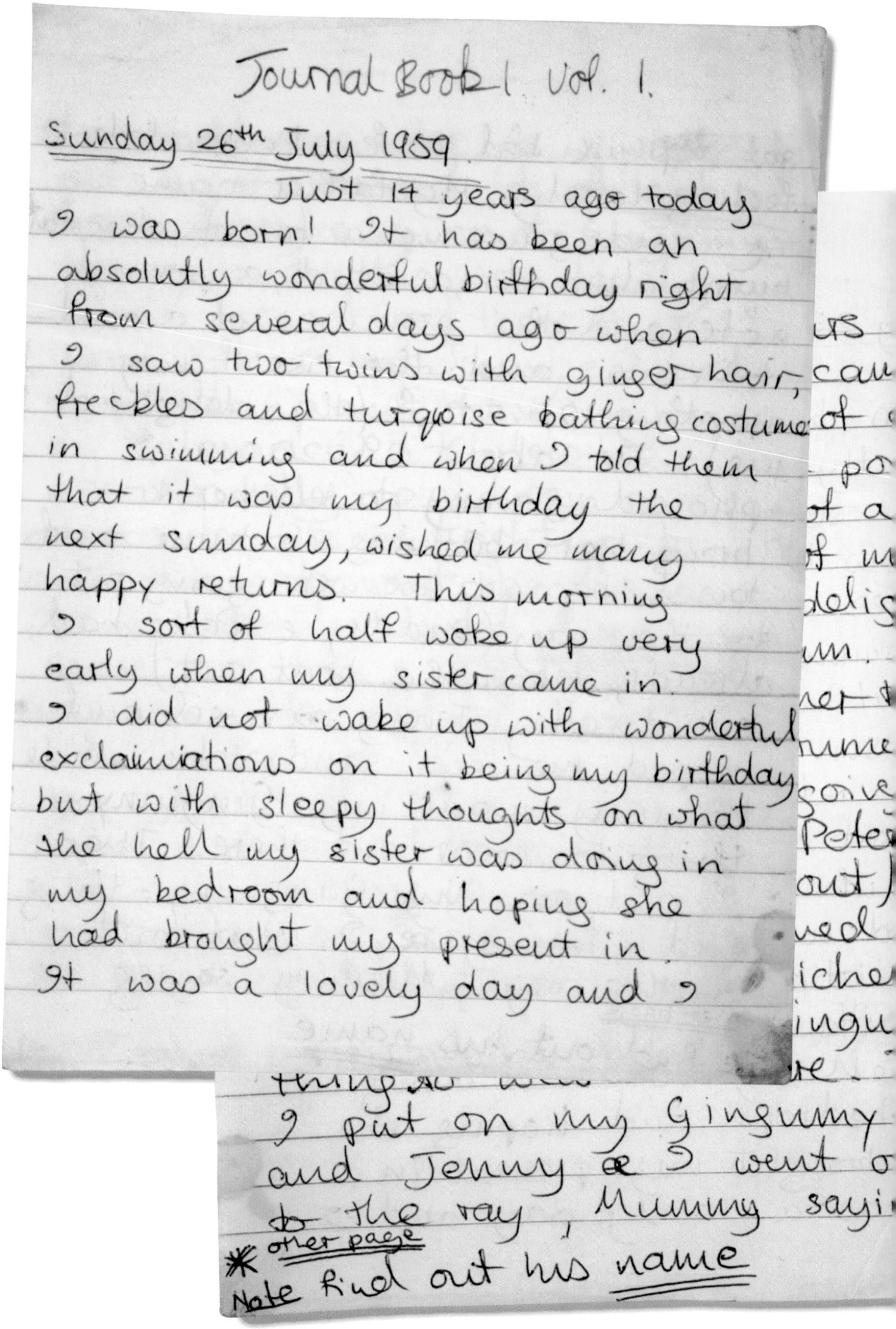

Journal Book 1. Vol. 1.

Sunday 26th July 1959.

       Just 14 years ago today I was born! It has been an absolutly wonderful birthday right from several days ago when I saw two twins with ginger hair, freckles and turqoise bathing costumes in swimming and when I told them that it was my birthday the next sunday, wished me many happy returns. This morning I sort of half woke up very early when my sister came in. I did not wake up with wonderful exclaimiations on it being my birthday but with sleepy thoughts on what the hell my sister was doing in my bedroom and hoping she had brought my present in. It was a lovely day and I

thing

I put on my gingumy and Jenny & I went o to the ray, Mummy sayi

※ other page
Note find out his name

us
cau
of
po
of a
of m
delig
um
ner
nume
somé
Peté
out)
ved
iche
ingu
re

Right: Jiving on the
seafront wearing that
'ginghamy thing' that
I thought was so cool.

she would come later. As we went
out I got lots and lots of looks
from everybody 'cos of ginghamy-
thing and this was lovely.
When we got out there it was
even better. ~~but~~ Jenny e I had
to parade up and down, waving
to Halcyon and Curlew who
were cruising up and down on the
other side. We went right up to
where the water went like this:—
(It was terribly crowded
there) and then
we saw Curlew
right miles up
the other end (where we had ~~been~~
before) and we had to run all
the way up there. (On the way
that nice boy* splashed me (s'os
I'd see him)). (I like him!) When we

Damn! one of the cards has fallen down!

Left and far left:
My first time on an
aeroplane was to visit
my first boyfriend, Jean
Louis, in Paris.
Below: Posing around
Southend.

I also tried to learn French, deeply impressed by the French boys who would turn up in Southend for the summer holidays, hoping to improve their English. I think they must have looked on the map, seen a seaside resort just down the road from London and imagined it was like St Tropez next to Paris. They must have had a horrible disappointment. However, the ones that I met were very sweet, and declared that HP sauce was the best thing they had ever tasted. Like all the other French boys, Jean Louis wore a blue Cashmere scarf around his neck and lovely navy blue sweaters and white shirts, looking impossibly chic amongst the Teds and Mods and rockers and general scruffiness that I was absolutely a part of. The French still wear those clothes, and amazingly they still look chic. And they still listen to Johnny Halliday. Are they mad?

Opposite: At St Bernard's,
third from the right,
third row down.

My best friend Jenny
and I did ballet
together for a while,
and then fell in love with all things French, especially
Brigitte Bardot. There is no relationship in your life
quite as intense as that first adolescent friendship,
sharing all dreams and pains without embarrassment.
We formed a group with Pattie and Mary, and the
four of us became, I am sure, a constant source of
irritation to nuns, teachers and fellow pupils alike, not
least because of our pretensions, which, like all teenagers,
we imagined were our invention. It was all Rimbaud
and Juliette Gréco, long hair de rigueur (at school we
had to tie it in plaits), if possible black stockings, and
gingham because that was what Bardot wore.

Opposite: Under the 'Longest Pier in the World'.
Below: Sailing on Dad's little boat, the *Curlew*. I never much took to sailing the grey cold waters of the Thames. I look fairly grumpy.

Teenage larking around had to end, with all its attendant tears into the pillow at night, and here are my sister and I off to college. She had gone a couple of years before me, and I think this must be my first day. A massive step into another world, but one I couldn't wait for.

I took these pictures of my home town. I have
always loved the atmosphere of an out-of-season
seaside resort.

# Starting Out

*With the National Youth Theatre – Cleopatra and getting an agent*

**It was Mrs Welding** who told me about the National Youth Theatre, an organisation I knew nothing about. She had spotted my love and maybe my potential, and gave me the pamphlet, and the application forms. Back then the Youth Theatre was run by Michael Croft as a sexist private fiefdom, creating a unique opportunity for young people from the kind of background that did not naturally lead to the theatre, to perform and learn. Happily, it still does. It was full of working-class kids from all over Britain. Every year, in the school summer holidays, the Youth Theatre would put on full productions, usually of Shakespeare, that would be reviewed by the national press. The plays Croft selected were invariably ones that required big crowds of young men: *Coriolanus*, *Henry V*, and *Julius Caesar*. There was a lot of running about and shouting.

I applied for an audition without telling anyone at school, I was so sure of rejection. I made the journey up to London with my dad, my second big audition accompanied by him. A few years earlier, at the age of thirteen or so, in my ballet phase, I had been invited to audition for the Royal Ballet School, and been turned down – thank God. I did Queen Margaret: 'Come, make him stand upon this molehill here…' a speech in which she taunts her opponent with a rag soaked in the blood of his dead son. I was mortified and deeply embarrassed by the horrible experience of having to audition in front of males. I had only ever acted in front of girls. I was seventeen, with all the physical shyness that infers. I tried desperately to overcome my mortification and gave it my all. I got in.

Dear, kind Auntie Gwen made it possible for me to go by letting me stay in her very small flat in Hampstead Road. It had a shared toilet and no bathroom. You had to wash standing in the kitchen in a bowl of water. A completely dangerous madman lived upstairs. It was perfect for me, because it made it possible for me to do this very exciting thing.

I only played a citizen, running and shouting with everyone else, but it was a start, and best of all it took place in a real theatre, the sadly destroyed Scala, just off Goodge Street, with a real stage door, real wings, real flies and a real auditorium. I vividly remember those dim, dusty wings, the ropes going high up into the darkness and the romance of the lit-up wooden stage. Just to walk through the entrance marked STAGE DOOR was thrilling. The physicality of the bricks and mortar of theatre was then and still is very important to me, and any theatre, even one that's empty, is full of meaning.

The next year I played Helena in *A Midsummer Night's Dream*. I was impressed by wearing a costume that had once been worn by Diana Rigg, already a famous actress. It had her name sewn in! I loved that little name tag. It made me feel like a professional. The following year I played Cleopatra and my career was launched.

In the meantime I had started my college studies in the New College of Speech and Drama, a teacher training college housed within Anna Pavlova's old home, Ivy House. This graceful villa on the Hampstead Road had a pond in the garden and two resident swans, à la *Swan Lake*. Anna Pavlova had been one of my heroines when I was in love with ballet. One night an audience showed their appreciation for her dancing by unhitching the horses from her troika and pulling it themselves, cheering, through the snowy streets of St Petersburg. Now that's a star! The welcoming speech as the new intake of students gathered for the first time in her old house commenced with a warning: if we wanted to act, we were in the wrong place. This college was only for teachers. My heart sank.

I had wanted to go to drama school, but my local council would not give grants for drama, art or music schools, thus making it economically impossible for me. So this was the next best thing, and it appealed to my parents, who wanted me to have something to fall back on. During my training, I taught in Bethnal Green Secondary Mod and it was abundantly clear that the teaching profession was not one I would excel in. My classes were mayhem.

It did give me an opportunity to discover the village nature of London, however. As a newcomer to the grand old city, I decided to teach a course on London architecture because it was something that impressed me. Midway through describing the architecture of Regent Street, I noticed puzzled looks on their faces. A hand went up.

'Where's Regent's Street, miss?'

'It's that big shopping street right in the middle of London. You know, the one that leads from Piccadilly Circus to Oxford Street.'

They hadn't heard of them either. I wondered if they were pulling my leg. This was a class of fifteen-year-olds, after all. Then, as I questioned them, it became clear that they had never been further west than Tottenham Court Road,

Queen's Theatre
one shilling

**The National Youth
Theatre**
**A MIDSUMMER
NIGHT'S DREAM**

The programme for *Midsummer Night's Dream*.

a couple of stops on the Underground. For them, that was 'going up West'. The rest of London was unknown territory; Chelsea might as well have been as far away as Manchester.

While at college I made wonderful friends, including Peter Freeman and his girlfriend Judy. Now known as Paul Freeman, he also became a successful actor. We had absolutely no money. I often went to bed wearing my coat as I could not afford to feed the gas-fire meter. Pubs cost money too, but at least they were warm and you could pretend to be drinking by getting lost in the crowd. There was also a coffee bar in Hampstead, called the Coffee Cup, where the owners kindly let you sit for hours with one cup of coffee.

My first digs comprised a room in a flat owned by a brave Jewish lady, who was very ill and needed to have oxygen every day. A lecturer at London University, hers was a brilliant mind in a twisted body. She was also the kindest person, putting up with me setting fire to her curtains by going out and leaving candles burning, and stealing a spoonful or two of cottage cheese from her fridge. She only threw me out when she started coming across strange boys in her corridor at one in the morning.

It was of course in London that I found sex, or rather it found me. It was not a wonderful discovery, or one sought out by me. It became the source of much heartache as I experienced the calumny of young men. I had arrived an innocent in mind and body, with very romantic notions that somehow sat side by side with my vehement feminism. It turned out to be a lethal mix. My trustful romantic nature was badly let down, my feminism confronted. I felt worthless and shamed, and became suspicious, hurt and angry, until I found someone who really cared for me. I am still pissed off, actually.

My next digs were a room in the attic of a tall building whose only bathroom was six flights down, with the ubiquitous meter for the hot water. I was living on my grant, which was tiny. It was hard enough to eat, let alone pay for hot water. As a supplement to my income I got a job as an usherette in the Everyman, an art cinema in Hampstead. I had a torch and a black dress. I loved both the costume and the role. There I got to see some of the greatest films of all time. In particular I remember *Citizen Kane*, which I saw many times.

After playing Cleopatra to some acclaim with the Youth Theatre I still had a year of college to go. I had an agent, and a job if I wanted. Quite a few repertory theatres had made enquiries. The question was whether to leave and start work in that real world. If I left college, it would mean I

Playing Kitty in *Charley's Aunt*, University Theatre, Manchester, 1969.

would have to pay back my grant. The thought of that debt terrified me, and foolishly I stayed on, even though it was clear by then that I was not destined to teach.

At this time I had the good luck to meet and go out with, and stay in with Ken Cranham, a fellow actor from the National Youth Theatre. It was Ken who restored my self-esteem and romantic tendencies. We loved each other. I found a person who shared my interests, and introduced me to more. He was so lovely to me and I am indebted to him. He saved me from a terminal rage. His family were kind-hearted and welcoming. His mother often cooked us a delicious Sunday lunch that was gratefully received. We would also dream about going to a good restaurant and ordering separate dishes. We had so little money we had to go to the cheapest Chinese or Indian place and share one bowl of the least expensive item on the menu. When Ken left college ahead of me and landed a job in the West End, in a Joe Orton play, he immediately took me to a posh Chinese restaurant, where we ordered more than one dish. It was fabulous.

Ken, like all the men I have had a proper relationship with, left me a better person than he found me. He took me to boxing matches; I remember going to Leicester Square at three in the morning to watch Muhammad Ali beat Sonny Liston on the big screen. It was an amazing night. Strangely, all my guys have loved boxing, good food and good music. We would also queue up for the gods at the Old Vic and see Olivier and Joan Plowright, Maggie Smith, Frank Finlay and Geraldine McEwan, in legendary performances. Ken once queued up all night for a ticket to see Olivier playing Othello, a famous performance. He got the ticket and then slept through the whole thing because he was so tired from being up all night. These productions and performances I remember very clearly. It was extraordinarily exciting, and fed into my ambitions of becoming a great stage actress. Nothing on the screen compared to it for me. I did love foreign films, however, and we would go to see Fellini, Antonioni, Renoir, Alain Renais and anything French.

Ken went to RADA, the illustrious drama school. I was jealous. The students seemed confident and sophisticated, even supercilious, and they had scripts under their arms. In retrospect, however, I'm very glad I did not go to drama school. I think that experience can destroy as much as it teaches. It is an intensely competitive environment, much more so than in the professional arena. I was left in the raw, so to speak, and my learning took place in the real world of theatre, acting with, watching, and therefore being taught by some of the best actors in Britain.

My first professional job was in Manchester at the University Theatre (which later became the Royal Exchange Theatre). After playing Cleopatra with the Youth Theatre I had been approached by agents who wanted to represent me. I was very lucky in this, as it's so often a catch-22 situation for actors: you can't get work without an agent, and you can't get an agent without working.

I signed with a darling man, Al Parker, an old-school American agent living in London and working with his wife, Maggie Parker, an ex-actress who by then was really running the agency. She approached agenting in a very motherly way. Whether you were eating healthily was as important as what role you were playing. Making money mattered less than making a career. She stayed my agent until she retired, many years later, and then I remained with her loyal assistant, Sandy Rees.

Maggie and Al sent me off for a couple of gruesome film auditions, one of which was with Michael Winner. He earned my eternal disdain and anger by

The telegram sent by Al Parker after seeing *Antony and Cleopatra*.

asking me to stand up and turn around, as if I was a slave in a market. It was humiliating, and even more humiliating was the fact that I did not have the balls to overturn his desk and tell him to bugger off. I never did that again.

In fact I wanted, and was destined for, the theatre. Apart from a rare brilliant excursion into the northern working class, British film at that time consisted largely of Hammer Horror and *Carry On*. Neither offered anything that excited me. More than anything, I wanted to be a Shakespearean stage actress, because that writer had seduced me and addicted me.

My first break came when I was approached by Braham Murray to join his company in Manchester, to play one of the girls in *Charley's Aunt* with the famous and successful actor Tom Courtenay. I spent a lot of time giggling at Tom's brilliant performance. And after that I played Nerina in *The Merchant of Venice*.

There was an actor from the old school in this company called Barry Cussins, a lovely man. He taught me a lot about acting. He had done twice-weekly rep just after the war, which meant having to rehearse, learn and perform two different plays every week. This inevitably led to all kinds of disasters, and he shared with me many of those great old theatre stories. This was really the start of my professional career, and it held all the delights of repertory theatre.

The first of these was the digs. Not so different from being a student: no heat, or at least, no money for the meter, and not much money for food. Breakfast at the digs consisted of mountains of wet white bread thinly spread with margarine. Our staple diet consisted of the most enormous and incredibly greasy spring rolls from the Chinese takeaway, which cost very little and filled you up for hours. However, there was the camaraderie, and the equality of an actors' ensemble, something all actors love and feel comfortable within. This I found and loved in Manchester, and again about six months later at Stratford-upon-Avon.

Before Stratford, one of the directors at the Youth Theatre asked me to play *Little Malcolm and His Struggle Against the Eunuchs*, a typical Angry Young Man play of the sixties. As with all those plays, it was a boy's fantasy and the girl's role was sexist crap. However, it was a professional engagement, with a wage attached. We played it for one week at the Empire, Sunderland. The vast, echoing mausoleum of an auditorium seated around two thousand. We attracted around two hundred. The seats of the theatre were like cinema seats; they flipped noisily up if anyone stood to leave. Many people took that option, especially when I had to deliver the line 'Will you shaft me?' By the end of the play there were maybe a hundred and thirty-four left in the audience.

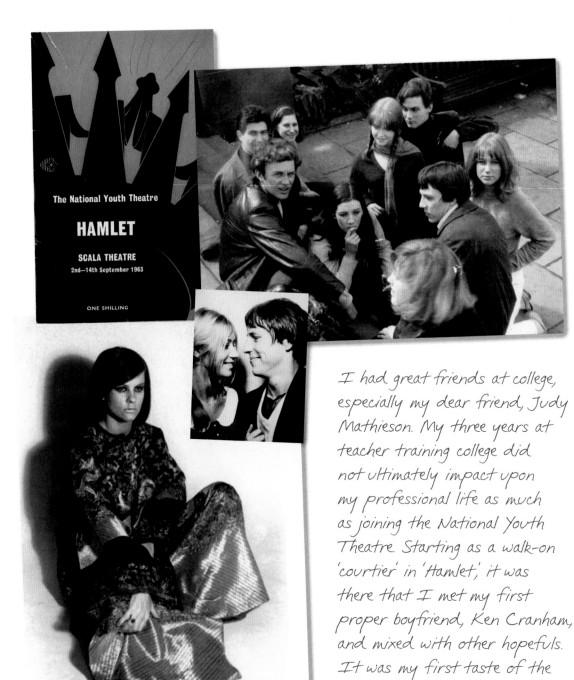

The National Youth Theatre

HAMLET

SCALA THEATRE
2nd—14th September 1963

ONE SHILLING

I had great friends at college, especially my dear friend, Judy Mathieson. My three years at teacher training college did not ultimately impact upon my professional life as much as joining the National Youth Theatre. Starting as a walk-on 'courtier' in 'Hamlet,' it was there that I met my first proper boyfriend, Ken Cranham, and mixed with other hopefuls. It was my first taste of the community of actors.

The following year I was asked to play Helena in 'A Midsummer Night's Dream'. Bad casting, as Helena is supposed to be tall and thin and I was short and fattish.
I was very excited because the costume had Diana Rigg's name sewn into it. She is tall and thin, and she was a famous actress. I felt I had arrived in the real world of acting, even though my costume didn't fit. Here Diana and I are both wearing the same costume.

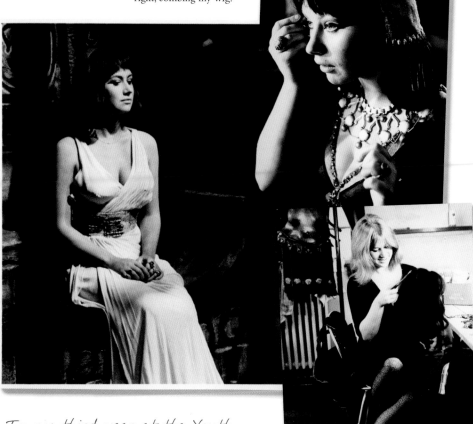

Right: Applying my make-up for Cleopatra, 1965; Below: On Cleopatra's throne; Opposite: A photograph taken during a break in rehearsals, and below right, combing my wig.

In my third year at the Youth Theatre I was asked to play Cleopatra. I had to overcome my toxic mix of a great physical shyness and a palpable physical presence. I was in an environment full of testosterone and chaotic male hormones, and the word sexist had not yet been invented. I was in at the deep end. I loved the power and the passion of that role, and of course, it's always good to be queen. I tried to ignore the real world and engage in the imaginative world of that great character. I had to do my own wig and make-up, of course. I also had a horrible flu for the whole of the one and only week we played at the Old Vic Theatre. This was the role that launched my career.

# Stratford

## *The Royal Shakespeare Company and a house called Parsenn Sally*

**I had been invited to audition** for the Royal Shakespeare Company, and duly did, and was given a place in that extraordinary and subsidised institution. Trevor Nunn had just taken over from Peter Hall. He was young, only twenty-seven, I believe, and looked eighteen, so he was regularly challenged by the security guard on his way to rehearsals.

It was the perfect time to join, the start of something new. My first role was as Castiza in the macabre Jacobean play, *Revenger's Tragedy*. It gave me a love for those Gothic, extreme plays of passion, murder and mayhem – sixteenth-century Quentin Tarantino, right up my alley. This was a spectacular production, all in black and white, very visual and with a sensational central performance by Ian Richardson, matched by the great Alan Howard. Castiza was not much of a role, all put-upon innocence, not the kind of thing I wanted to play, but a central role, and a wonderful way to start.

In fact, the whole experience was a wonderful way to start. The theatre was big and vocally demanding, so I was in at the deep end there. We had a voice teacher, Kate Fleming, followed by the famous Cicely Berry; and above all we had rehearsals. The repertory system means you rehearse at day and perform at night, different plays. Sometimes we would rehearse one play in the morning, perform another play in the afternoon and another one at night, all great pieces of literature. Around this time, my relationship with Ken came to an end, unable to withstand the pressure of my putting work before love.

At night we would fall into the Black Swan pub, otherwise known as the Dirty Duck, for a lock-in that would last until three or four in the morning. Then I would head home through the low fog that rises on the Avon as the sun rises. The Dirty Duck is the only pub I have ever loved. It was run at that time by a powerhouse called Pam, who knew the most intimate details about every actor, both professional and personal. She was a tyrant and a mother confessor, an amazing woman in body and personality, and she took no shit from anyone. It was the place you could bang on about the audience, about why this scene worked and that one didn't, and about what was going on in the rehearsal room, ad nauseam.

You could joke and you could flirt. You could laugh until you cried and then cry until someone made you laugh again. After a performance, actors need a space to unwind. It is physically and mentally impossible to go straight to bed when you come off stage. Like everyone else, actors need to complain, gossip and crack jokes. The only trouble is that they get off work at eleven at night. The Dirty Duck performed a great service for many years before me and many years after. Its walls must resound with the passions of thousands of performers, actors and dancers, for the Royal Ballet would do a season there as well. Pam told me that the dancers were even bigger drinkers than the actors.

As ever, I found a room in what must have been the last remaining building in Stratford without a proper bathroom or running hot water. It didn't matter too much because it was in a beautiful old Elizabethan building, full of atmosphere, and I had the theatre just across the street. I earned very little that first year, being the lowest of the low in wage terms. Once again, barely enough to eat, and not enough to spend money in the pub, so alcohol did not feature in my life. Nights in the Duck consisted of sitting with one warm drink for hours. It was quite a few years before I could drink much more than a glass or two without being dizzy or sick.

On stage as Cressida.

In the company was an actor called Bruce Myers who made me laugh and became my partner. Bruce came from a large excitable Jewish family based in Manchester, and I found them very liberating and great fun to be around. Although I was not Jewish they showed me warmth and made me welcome. Some of his family are still very close friends.

I think it was in my second year at Stratford that I met up with a group of people who would become very good friends for the rest of my life when I visited a house called Parsenn Sally. Though Sarah Ponsonby's home has often mistakenly been described as a commune, it was in truth simply a house that was shared by a group of friends, like a flat share in London, except in the country. It was an artists' haven, visited by musicians, painters, jugglers, gardeners, horse trainers, actors, furniture makers, property developers, designers, rich people and poor people, and general hangers-on.

The central character, the queen bee whose house it was, was Sarah. Here was and is one of the most extraordinary people I have ever met. A painter and prankster, with a mind like a trap, a posh girl who can do *The Times* crossword in about five minutes, with the most fertile imagination. Actually it was quite terrifying, but also incredible fun, and for me a necessary antidote to the seriousness of my struggle to become an actress.

The house was like a cross between a country weekend for toffs, an artists' convention, and a travellers' camp. There was constant dressing up, animals everywhere, champagne occasionally and, if not, gallons of wine, games of wit always, lots of music. The music was Santana, Crosby Stills and Nash, Pink Floyd, Led Zeppelin, and Randy Newman. There were often intimidating competitions, usually to do with wordplay. No mercy was shown to slowcoaches. The boys loved dressing in drag and the girls as nuns or tarts. There were also drugs, of course, marijuana mostly. Anyone who came was seduced, including some disapproving and uptight characters who hours later would be seen running through the garden with a feather boa round their neck. It was just irresistible. A scruffy Marie-Antoinette-meets-Ken Kesey existence. There were also serious conversations, good food always and dressing for dinner. Preparing dinner was a shared thing; it never seemed to be a problem. Likewise washing up. Certainly it was where I learned to cook for twelve people (something I've since forgotten). There were occasional rows about money and who owed what, usually related to the telephone, but nothing serious. Sex was private and personal, and almost always between established partners. There was a sweetness and kind of prudish innocence about it all, at least whenever I was around. My first night there I shared a bed with a large hairy Irish gentleman in the form of an Irish wolfhound called Murphy, who was outraged that I had been given his bed. He spent the night trying to oust me, sometimes successfully.

Because I was working flat out at Stratford, just down the road, I never actually lived at Parsenn Sally. This Victorian farmhouse, rented at a peppercorn rate from a posh friend of Sarah's who needed the place to be occupied, had been decorated with murals and the colours of the Caribbean and named after a cow Sarah knew. It was imaginative, it was beautiful. I had never seen anything like it. It was also always dirty for the animals held sway, treated as equals with the humans. It was a place you could find peace and privacy if you wanted, an intense conversation with a retired general, or a cat, or a raucous game of 'Postman' which involved much shouting and running about, delivering letters.

Later, Sarah moved to Wiltshire and a ruin of a house called Surrendell. The menagerie of animals and humans went with her, and I visited her there too. Even later, she decamped to France and took the geese across the Channel in a decommissioned London taxi. When I visited Surrendell the bedrooms had not yet been built, and we slept in great comfort in the haystack. This was the house that Princess Margaret would later visit. She was a friend of Roddy Llewellyn who was, like me and many others, a sometime weekend visitor. I heard of her impending visit, for there was much excitement about it in the aristocratic heart of the place. However I made sure I was well away, not wanting to be a part of all that and foreseeing the fuss that might ensue. Contrary to reports, I never met her there, and indeed never met her anywhere except a couple of times in formal situations related to the theatre.

After Bruce, my next partner was George Galitzine, the ex step-brother to Sarah and still a beloved friend. He balanced my shyness with his gregariousness, and laughter. All the men I have been with above all made me laugh. Georgie's full title is Prince George Galitzine, his family having been honoured for a forefather bonking Catherine the Great. Like me, George is half Russian, but from an aristocratic family that had the sense to escape the Bolsheviks with money. There are a lot of Russian princes and princesses. Catherine was generous with her favours.

George was by then the ex-boyfriend of another friend from those days, Sandy Campbell. She was one of the most upbeat, lively and quick-witted people I had ever known, and the only one who could and did beat Sarah at a mean game of backgammon. She was also very pretty, like Twiggy and with the same legs that never give up. Sandy, George and Sarah are still my very good friends, with Sandy also now fulfilling the role of my PA. Next to my sister she is the closest person to me, and I am godmother to one of her sons.

The green and the gold of the English countryside were like a drug for me. I would stand transfixed by the beauty and the smells. The soft damp smell of distant fungus, the dry crackly smell of wheat in June, the strange pungent smells of the wild flowers, the richness of the ploughed earth. A single tree in a field could stick me to the spot. One of the lowest parts of Britain, the area would be wreathed in those magical low mists that rise from the river or the field, making a landscape of mystery and fairies. It was the first time I had been exposed to real countryside, real nature. My parents had no car while I lived at home, so trips to the countryside were not on. The stretches of Essex between London and Southend – those few sad fields after Dagenham and before Basildon – were all I had seen; not exactly sylvan.

And every day I was exposed to the brilliant poetic writing of a genius who had lived in and loved that landscape, that river, maybe some of those very trees. Shakespeare wrote so descriptively and recognisably about Warwickshire. It was splendid to watch the landscape change in smell, colour and texture as the season progressed and the farmworkers did their thing, made me feel as if I never wanted to leave Stratford.

I worked at Stratford, with seasons in London, for four years, and began to play some fairly major roles. All this time I took my job very seriously, keenly aware of my part in an important art form. I was helped in this by being surrounded by some of the greatest stage actors and actresses in Britain, many of whom were my contemporaries. I would stand in the wings and watch in awe. Frances De La Tour could make an audience laugh by doing absolutely nothing. The beautiful Susan Fleetwood, who so sadly died too soon and too young of cancer, lit up the stage with her energy. Alan Howard soared to heights of invention and poetic naturalism that were extraordinary. When he was on form there was no one like him, no one. He is the greatest classical actor I have known.

Then there was the experience of hearing the same language night after night, and the way Shakespeare works, finding some new meaning every time. Simply to hear the reiteration of a line of beauty and complexity was to find a kind of belief. The theatre became my religion and I wanted to serve it.

One actor in particular was encouraging and kind. Ian Richardson, one of the leading actors in Britain, shared his tremendous knowledge and craft so generously with me. I had one scene with him in *All's Well*. A comic genius on stage, he helped me get as many laughs as possible, and showed me how to get an exit round. When I got applause, he religiously waited for it to die down when he could easily have stopped it dead. He was a very dear man and he and his wife Maroussia showed me great kindness.

Lindy, Sandy, Bob and myself enjoying the sunshine and strawberries.

Drenched in that kind of hothouse atmosphere of theatre culture, where everyone else is living and breathing the work, I became more and more serious about what I perceived as my inadequacies, and worked to overcome them. This meant I was often to be seen walking along the river muttering my lines to myself. I would stand at the foot of the statue of Shakespeare by the river in Stratford and beg for inspiration, and enough breath.

During my second year at Stratford I was asked to appear in a film, *Age of Consent*, to be shot in Australia starring James Mason, with Michael Powell directing. The fact that my agent also represented James I am sure had a lot to do with my casting. I was given the time off from the schedule with the RSC, or maybe it just worked out, and off I flew to Australia via Hawaii. At this point in time I had only been on an aeroplane once before, when I flew to Paris to see Jean Louis and his family.

I was also asked by Peter Hall to play Hermia in his film version of *Midsummer Night's Dream*, so I was gaining film experience, but I did not let it interfere with my desire to continue learning about stage acting. At the end of each film, I presented myself back at the gates of the RSC, hoping for a good role.

And I was given some good roles, but never the ones I wanted. I longed to play Juliet for example, but was never asked. I did play Cressida in *Troilus and Cressida*, but in spite of it being a 'title role' it is underwritten. I also played some wimpy goody-goodies, Hero, for example. I felt frustrated.

There were compensations, however. With the RSC I had the opportunity to travel quite extensively. During my four years, I went on one of the first cultural exchanges to Russia, a one-night-stand tour around Europe, and a tour to America that took in Los Angeles, Detroit and San Francisco. This was all very exciting to me. Touring with a company of actors is a very romantic thing to do, especially if you love the company of actors as I do. There is a lot of childish behaviour, a lot of laughter and a lot of late nights in bars or restaurants. It was amazing, too, to be in those exotic places not as a tourist but as someone hopefully contributing to the culture.

Going to Russia was particularly significant for me, for obvious reasons. Before I went, my father gave me strict instructions not to mention my Russian roots or to attempt to find any relatives. He was aware of the potential danger, not to me but to them. At this time, Russia was out of the horrors of Stalinism but deep into the Cold War. This was a time of espionage; suspicion and an ongoing propaganda battle that I think we actors were a part of. Both sides seemed to view our arrival as something they could exploit. It was the time of Philby, Burgess and Blunt.

It was a moving moment for me when the plane touched down in Moscow. We flew Aeroflot, of course, and they were still using prop planes. It took hours to get there. From the moment we landed I walked around looking for my Russian nature to manifest itself. To a certain extent it did. I was asked directions in the street because I looked Russian. Also I was bending over backwards not to be prejudiced about the world I saw, my father's left-wing ideology echoing in my head. However the reality was that it was grim and unhappy. Old women would shout at you in the street if you crossed the road in the wrong place, laughter seemed to be unacceptable, and the shops had rows of the same thing. I had no idea before going to Soviet Russia how much of a Western consumer I had become, how addicted to variety and colour, and the fun of advertising.

Having no concept of rates of exchange, Bruce, my then boyfriend, and I had made the mistake of taking our earnings in Russian roubles. We made that decision because British currency could only be spent in the foreign hotel shops and restaurants, and we wanted to be out with the people of Russia. But the exchange rate was so dire that we could hardly afford to eat, let alone drink. Desperate for some kind of alcoholic enjoyment, we went off to buy some Russian brandy to keep us warm in the Moscow midwinter. We found the shop, with difficulty, and joined the very long queue of bundled-up Russians. We must have waited for at least an hour, slowly making our way forward across the cold tiled floor. Eventually we reached the counter, pointed and handed over our carefully saved roubles. The bottle was wrapped in brown paper and handed to me. I turned and took one step. The bottle slipped straight out of the bottom of the paper on to the floor and smashed. The whole long queue looked at me in silence with an indescribable expression of resignation and sympathy and understanding, but letting me know I was on my own. Very Russian.

Later Bruce went out with some students, got drunk and came back to the hotel, packed up all his clothes, including his boots and coat, and gave them to the students. He was left with nothing to wear for a week or so, freezing in the 20° below temperature of a Russian winter. No wonder I loved him.

Our American trip was equally interesting, as we arrived in 1967, the Summer of Love. Los Angeles was hit by some of the worst rainstorms on record during the six weeks we were there. I don't think we saw any sunshine, and houses were tumbling off hillsides, lending the city an apocalyptic quality.

After LA we moved to San Francisco, the epicentre of peace and love in the late sixties, and I saw my first hippies, and bought my first beads. In fact, although I loved the 'peace and love, man' and flower power side of hippydom, I hated the 'mother earth' role allocated to the women. Those soppy girls with their drippy hair and droopy clothes and baby on the hip irritated me. I was more attracted to the laughing, raucous, hell-raising, feather-wearing Janis Joplin, and her unforgettable voice.

After San Francisco we had three days before we were due in Detroit, and some of us took the option of travelling across America by train. This was a brilliant choice, and in those three days I felt I learned much about the American Dream and all the sacrifices in its name. The scale of the landscape was incredible to me, coming from the contained nature of the English countryside. It took a whole day to cross one plain, with no trees, or towns on it. The train would stop right in the main street of towns like Cheyenne and you could get off and dash into a bar and meet the locals for twenty minutes before getting back on board. The bar on the train would open and close at strange hours, according to the rules of whichever state we were travelling through.

Finally we arrived in Detroit, the place I loved the best, although it was by far the least glamorous. It was suffering from the effects of the riots that had happened just a few months before. However it was the first time I had been in a predominantly black community which had money. The shops were full of people spending and having fun. I went with another actor to a concert where we were the only white people in the audience. It got a bit hairy when one of the acts seemed to consist of a guy just shouting 'burn, whitey, burn' to a drum beat. The audience however treated us with complete graciousness. I also met up with a beautiful American football player, also black, who took me to some fantastic music clubs. One we had to leave hastily as there grew a sense of

Good friends then and now: Terry Taplin, George Galitzine, Sarah Ponsonby, Murphy the dog, me and Andrew Saunders.

animosity towards us from the girls there. I was scared. They were going to 'kick my butt'.

The huge Diego Rivera murals in the town hall, so overtly pro worker, were astounding for that capitalist country. Detroit was not pretty, but to me it seemed beautiful and at that time I much preferred it to San Francisco or Los Angeles.

Work carried on at the RSC with many different productions, many different roles. One of the advantages of regular employment was that, on paper, it made you look like a responsible person to those in the financial world. I took advantage of this and bought my first house, at last having saved enough money for the deposit. I bought it together with my old friend Terry Taplin and his girlfriend, Lindy. We were to share the house, them upstairs and me downstairs. At that time you could not get a joint mortgage without being engaged to be married, so Terry and I went through an overacted pantomime as an engaged couple for the benefit of the mortgage lenders. It involved sitting on knees, I seem to remember. We got our mortgage, and the three of us moved into a respectable working-class part of London called Parsons Green. We promptly painted the red-brick house green and yellow, all over, like a Jamaican house. Over the next eighteen years we watched the area turn into the expensive exclusive part of London it now is.

After four years of work and travel, rehearsal and performance with the RSC, I began to feel as if I was walking on the spot, or rather gently making a wheel of tasteful culture go round and round.

Things were moving and shaking in the world of theatre by this time. Actors were questioning the very shape of theatre, asking why did it have to be performed in a theatre at all, or from a written text. In the States the Living Theater and La MaMa were throwing the whole thing up in the air and in Europe Grotowski was experimenting with the psychology of theatre. Actors wanted smaller, more intimate spaces. Fringe theatre was on the rise.

Back then, there was no small space in Stratford. That came later out of the move by a group of actors and trainee directors, including Mike Leigh and Mark Rylance, to borrow a small space in the gardens at Stratford. Much to the annoyance of the bureaucracy, they made their own theatre there where Mike Leigh experimented with his first improvised theatre, Mark devised plays, and Ben Kingsley did a brilliant impersonation of Peter Brook.

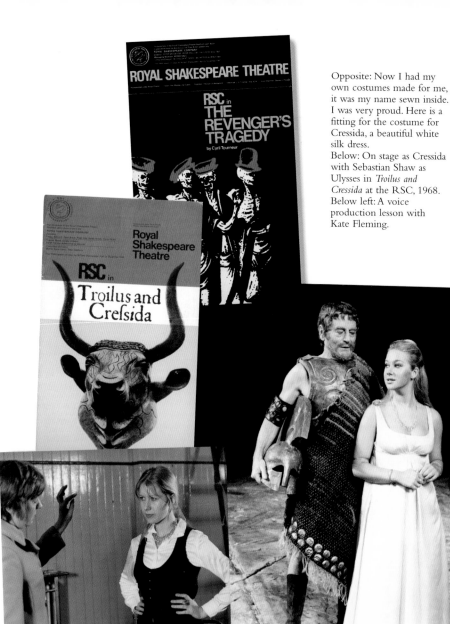

ROYAL SHAKESPEARE THEATRE

RSC in
THE
REVENGER'S
TRAGEDY
by Cyril Tourneur

Royal
Shakespeare
Theatre

RSC in
Troilus and
Cressida

Opposite: Now I had my
own costumes made for me,
it was my name sewn inside.
I was very proud. Here is a
fitting for the costume for
Cressida, a beautiful white
silk dress.
Below: On stage as Cressida
with Sebastian Shaw as
Ulysses in *Troilus and
Cressida* at the R.S.C, 1968.
Below left: A voice
production lesson with
Kate Fleming.

After Manchester
I joined the Royal
Shakespeare Company. My first two roles were Castiza
in 'Revenger's Tragedy' and Cressida in 'Troilus and
Cressida'. I was not really ready for this but steamed
ahead anyway, helped by kind and experienced actors like
Sebastian Shaw, Norman Rodway, and especially Ian
Richardson. Ian took me under his wing, showed me
respect and taught me with generosity. He and his wife
Maroussia were so kind, I shall never forget it.

In the long wait in 'Hamlet' after the mad scene
and before the gravedigger scene, my friend Barry
Stanton and I would get up to mischief. He
was playing the gravedigger and I was Ophelia.
I liked to haunt the roof of the theatre at
Stratford, in my death make-up. I would
wander up and down, hoping a tourist would
catch sight of me and think I was a ghost.
Barry and I also invented a story of Ophelia
and the gravedigger being madly in love, a tragic
story that ends with both their deaths.

I did many roles in my time with the RSC, in a variety of plays. It was a great time of learning, not just about acting, but also about literature and history. Those years gave me an everlasting love of the ensemble.

## Arriving in Australia

When I was cast in *Age of Consent* I had never worked on film and had only travelled on an aeroplane once before. I was very excited, I was to be paid a lot of money in comparison to the measly amount I was earning at the Royal Shakespeare Company. That money was burning a hole in my pocket. I decided to go to that enemy territory, the King's Road, to buy myself an outfit wear to travel to Australia. I bought a short brown leather skirt and a bomber jacket to match. I spent more than I had ever spent before, all of my clothes at that time coming from charity shops and jumble sales. I was delivered to Heathrow to take the plane to Honolulu. There I was to be met, given some *per diem*, and taken to a hotel to meet James Mason, stay the night and then travel on to Sydney the next day. The plane ride was incredible. Qantas was a young airline, eager to impress and I was travelling first class, the only person in first class. The stewardesses treated me with great care, plying me with champagne.

We arrived in Honolulu at about two in the morning, the last plane to arrive. I stepped off the plane in my leather outfit, saw my first palm tree and was instantly drenched in sweat. It was so HOT! And humid! In the terminus were people meeting people off the plane with leis made of the sweet-smelling plumeria, which they hung around the necks of their friends. I waited for my lei. No one arrived. Slowly the terminus emptied out, until I was the only person left, with my bags and very hot in my King's Road suit, and somewhat overhung. I had no money, nowhere to stay and I simply did not know what to do. I started snivelling. Then I saw a sign that said 'lost and found' It was over the only office open in the airport. I considered my situation. The sign seemed to suit it.

I walked in and saw something straight out of *In the Heat of the Night*: a cop, substantially over-weight, with sweat under his arms staining his shirt, his gun on his hip and his feet on the desk. He asked me what he could do for me. I said I was lost and needed to be found. He asked me to tell him the whole story. I said I thought I was booked into a hotel somewhere in Honolulu. He got on the phone. I was booked into the Hilton, the first one he called. He then took me to his police car, that was just like in the movies, and put the flashing light on and the siren, and drove me at 100 miles an hour to the hotel. It was a great arrival.

I was shown into a vast suite and fell asleep, exhausted. In the morning, not quite knowing where I was, I stumbled to the shutters and opened them. Before me was the magnificent blue Pacific and more palm trees gently swaying in the balmy breeze. I let out a yell that awoke James Mason in his suite next door. We then had breakfast together on the terrace facing the ocean and I was introduced to the truly glamorous and sybaritic side of the film world.

Top: There is nothing like a printed business card to make the ephemeral real.

Here are James Mason and myself in 1969 on the wild beach of Dunk
Island, one of the islands off the Great Barrier Reef of Australia.
I had to learn to free dive for this film, and worked up to being
able to spend quite a long time under water. While in Sydney,
preparing, I had been given the use of a pool to train. A wealthy
couple owned this pool. The wife was quite young and charming.
One day, I was practising in the pool when suddenly two enormous
dogs bounded up. I heard the words 'Rommel, Goering, come here!'
uttered in a German accent. I looked up and silhouetted against
the sun was a tall grey-haired man, maybe about sixty years old
I got out as fast as I could and never went back. James and
I went native doing this film. We stopped wearing shoes and formal
clothes. We caused a scandal when we returned to civilisation. The
good people of Townsville thought we were insulting them by appearing
like a couple of savages.

Following pages: From my scrapbook. The house and the inhabitants of Parsenn Sally.

Above left: One of the
hundreds of dinners for
ten or more that we
enjoyed. Left: Sarah with
Murphy, the dog who
selfishly would not give
up his bed for me.
Above: Me with my then
boyfriend George
Galitzine.

Life at Parsenn Sally, near
Stratford, was drugs and rock and
roll and also dressing for dinner and
backgammon. It was called a commune
by journalists, but in reality was far
from that. More a house shared by
friends, a cross between a travellers'
encampment and a posh country house.

Following pages: George's
painting of the fireplace at
Parsenn Sally. It perfectly
describes the house. It was
also my mother's favourite
picture.

The start of my one and only acid
trip, a walk in the country. I am
laughing already. And the end result.
A commune with nature.

# Stratford's very own sex queen

A profile of Helen Mirren by Philip Oakes; photograph by Colin Jones

Helen Mirren bombs through Stratford-upon-Avon in a white MG, the top down, her blonde hair loosely tethered by a scarf. She's wearing a home-made granny skirt (black with mauve stripes), and a rather sorry black sweater. She has a cold, and because she's forgotten to bring any tissues, she dabs at her nose with a sodden clump of paper napkins swiped from a restaurant.

She looks, to put it kindly, a bit frayed. But her effect on the populace is extraordinary. Road-menders whistle. Shoppers smile. A man with a ladder narrowly misses stabbing the end through a window. At a snarled-up junction the traffic cop halts the oncoming lane and waves her by. Miss Mirren is the Royal Shakespeare Company's very own sex queen, and the legend has taken hold.

It has not really been of her making. All that she's done is be herself, a nicely-rounded girl who plays plum female roles – Cleopatra, Cressida, and Ophelia to name the top three – and says candid things about sex which most other girls also think but rarely get the chance to utter. She's a very good actress, but it's not her technique that has brought the critics out in a flux of superlatives. "Sensual", "graceful", "buxom", "especially telling in projecting the woman's sluttish eroticism" are the phrases they've used to describe her. The publicists publicise. Audiences respond with a massive wave of wish-fulfilment, and an image is born.

An interesting aspect of the phenomenon is that most of the fans who wait for her at the stage door of the Memorial Theatre are women. What's the attraction, one wonders. They're friendly, admiring, but there's no trace of that butch fervour which so often marks the Ladies Paddock in the gallery. There are usually one or two schoolgirls, mums on an outing, and possibly a W.I. group paying homage before the coach-trip home.

It's doubtful, in fact, whether it is homage at all. What Helen Mirren embodies is a kind of unbuttoned niceness, a dream of warm and essentially wholesome flesh. She's emancipated, unmarried, a citizen of that best of all possible worlds in which freedom, success, and responsibility are reconciled. Most ➤➤➤

resident. What unsettles Helen Mirren, however, is not Stratford's insu-larity, but the emotional transience [it] breeds. "It's a very treacherous place. [It's] so beautiful, so green that it en-[clo]ses you. An affair here is completely [en]capsulated. You have to hang on to [yo]ur cool."

How long she'll stay is a matter for [spe]culation. This year she turned [do]wn the lead part in the new film of [*Wu*]*thering Heights* (it went, she's [hap]py to say, to her friend, Anna [Ca]lder Marshall), but she knows that [eve]ntually she's bound to take the [plu]nge away from Stratford and into [con]temporary drama. She's properly [app]rehensive: "Tackling a new role [ma]kes me feel sick. I realise that I [spe]nd a great deal of my life concen-[trat]ing on being non-neurotic."

She's a hard worker, hugely ambi-[tiou]s, trusting to a remarkable degree [on] her director to steer her where [she]'s likely to do her best work. Before [play]ing Ophelia she'd seen only two [pro]ductions of *Hamlet* – the TV film [star]ring Christopher Plummer and an [ama]teur production at Southend. She [like]s to work instinctively, but dur-[ing] rehearsals her Ophelia became [mou]lded largely by the director, [Tre]vor Nunn. "That's your best [beh]aviour position," he told her as [she] perched stiffly on a stool to sing [a d]uet with Hamlet. And instantly [her] shoulders drooped, the poker [oo]zed out of her spine.

[S]he's no-one's dummy, though. [She] has reservations about Michael [Pow]ell, who directed *Age of Consent* [beca]use, it seems, he shouted a lot. [I d]idn't like that. When I'm bullied, [I te]nd to stick out my chin and fight [back]."

[M]ost of her friends, she says, are [othe]r actresses. "I don't mind the competition a bit. It's perfectly natural. What I can't stand is when a woman comes into a room with just one thought in her tiny mind: what effect she's having on the men."

The sex-queen bit is something she finds tiresome, although she understands that, in its gentlemanly way, the RSC must help it along because, after all, their business is show business. Also, she's come to realise, her brand of sensuality is a very uncommon property, and not to use it, either aesthetically or commercially, would be an appalling waste.

She's stuck with it then, not glumly, but a trifle resignedly. She still wants to be a great actress, which is not – you might say – the way of all flesh, only that of prime quality. "Actresses can't be ordinary people," she says, cutting a corner in that white MG. "They have to be different. I can see that now. Acting is such an un-natural thing to do." ●

*This article came out in a Sunday supplement and the headline was to haunt me for the next twenty years or more. I shall never forgive Mr Oakes. The car referred to in this piece was an absolute lemon sold to me by my brother. The engine exploded after I'd had it a week. It was true that at that time I turned down film roles to concentrate on theatre.*

*Opposite: This picture was done by my friend then boyfriend then friend again, the artist George Galitzine.*

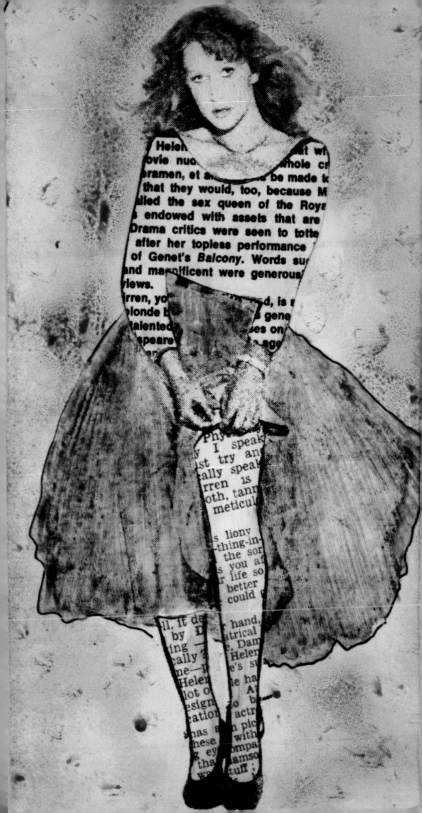

Helen ... at wl
ovie nud ... whole cr
ramen, et a ... be made to
that they would, too, because M
lled the sex queen of the Roya
endowed with assets that are
Drama critics were seen to totte
after her topless performance
of Genet's *Balcony*. Words su
nd magnificent were generous
iews.
rren, yo ... d, is
londe b ... gene
talented ... es on
speare ... age

Phy ...
I speak
st try an
cally speak
rren is
oth, tann
meticul

liony
thing-in
the sor
s you a
r life so
better
could

ll, it de ... hand,
by D ... t ... atrical
ing — ... e, Dam
cally ... Helen
me—R ... e's sv
Helen ... le ha
lot o ... A
esign ... o b
ation ... actri
has ... picl
hese ... with
g ey ... mpa
tha ... amso
wa ... tuff

Camping on the beach at Eilat.

## On the Kibbutz

After a stint at the RSC and travelling in the States, Bruce, still my partner at that time, decided that we should visit Israel. As a Jew, his culture and history called him there. He suggested that we go together to work on a kibbutz for a couple of weeks, which I thought was a great idea.

And so we arrived, two very green but keen 'tourists' as the kibbutzim accurately called any visitors. It was about five months after the end of the Six-Day War, so decisively won by the Israelis. Ha'on, the kibbutz we had arranged to visit and work on, was a rural commune that grew grapes, amongst other things. Its vines nestled into the hills of the Golan Heights, the location for much fighting in the war. The Heights had just been occupied by the Israelis and there was still some shelling.

After a day to recover from the journey, I was to present myself for work. I was assigned to a young kibbutznik and sent out at 5 a.m. into the grapevines. They were a few miles from the community itself. I had been given a big plastic comb and was told literally to comb the grapes. This was to take off the smaller grapes to make room for the others to grow big. These grapes were destined for the table.

On the way out in the truck the young man told me how much he hated Arabs and wanted to join the army and kill them. He was about seventeen.

I was horrified. This did not fit into my understanding of the idealism of the kibbutz. However, I kept my thoughts to myself, determined to be a good 'Tourist'. He sent me off into the vines with my comb and made his way down the other end. From time to time I would hear him speaking in Hebrew on his walkie-talkie.

After an hour or so I suddenly heard the inimitable high-pitched whine of a shell coming my way. It had been launched from the Syrian side and I looked up to see a puff of white smoke on the hillside, falling in the vines. The sound of the conversation being carried on with the base got louder and more intense. I carried on combing, thinking that this was what the kibbutz had to put up with and I had better be brave. More whines, and more puffs of smoke, getting closer, more shouting into the walkie-talkie.

Eventually, around 11.30 a.m. it was time to go back to base for lunch. In that heat you start work early and finish early, to do more later in the afternoon.

We arrived back to find Ha'on in uproar. The base had been ordering the young man back and he had been refusing, saying he was a brave Israeli soldier, and would not back down in the face of the enemy. The rest of the kibbutz, including Bruce, had been in the bomb shelter all morning, even though the bombs had been falling far from them. It was the first time this particular kibbutz had come under fire.

The next day I was taken off grape-combing duties and assigned to the kitchen. This was the communal kitchen that every day fed about two hundred people. I was taken to a far corner and shown a huge pile of very greasy pans that needed to be washed. I set to work, and as I washed more pans were added to the pile. Behind me was the clatter and noise of a large kitchen. I slowly worked my way through the pile, making my own loud clatter. As I finally reached the end of the pile, some hours later, it dawned on me that everything had gone very quiet behind me. I turned around and realised that the kitchen was completely deserted. I was still standing there perplexed, wondering what to do next, when a woman came dashing in and indicated that I should follow her. Once again the shelling had driven the rest of the kibbutz down into the shelter. Some time had passed before they realised they'd left me in the corner.

Bruce then decided we might be safer hitch-hiking and camping out around Israel, which we did.

# Peter Brook

## *Experimental theatre – touring the world*

**In 1970, the already legendary Peter Brook** did his famous production of *Midsummer Night's Dream*. I had very much wanted to play Titania in that production, but Peter rightfully gave the role to Sara Kestelman, who was dazzling in it. I only got to understudy Hermia, but had the advantage of being around for much of the rehearsal period, and watching the whole thing come to the extraordinary life it had. It is still being copied, or 'homaged'.

I had seen Brook's production of *The Tempest* at the Roundhouse in London and loved the way he redrew the relationship of audience and actor. Actor became audience and the audience would find themselves part of the play. This was all new. I then heard that Peter was preparing a new company of international actors, to work experimentally in Paris. It was what I wanted to do. I wanted to throw it all out and start again. I asked Brook if he would consider me, and he said I could go to Paris to see how it worked out. Bruce also applied, but whereas he could go immediately, I had the remaining year of my contract to work out. I also had been cast by Lindsay Anderson to play in *O Lucky Man!* which was to be shot in London.

My agent, family and most fellow actors thought I was mad to consider the move to Paris. As far as my family were concerned I had a nice regular job in a respected company doing great work, in a profession where all was uncertain. As far as my agent was concerned I was just getting known, articles were appearing in newspapers about me, and film and television roles were being offered, as well as other theatre. And I was about to walk away from all that. To them it seemed like professional suicide, but I was determined. There was no question, this was what I wanted. As soon as I could, I went to Paris and turned up on the doorstep of the Mobilier National, the ancient tapestry factory in Paris, where Peter had been given the top floor by the Cultural Ministry.

I almost missed my chance by being totally disorganised. I had failed to let the company know that I was finally free and coming. When I called to announce that I was on my way, I was told not to bother, I'd missed the opportunity. I said I would come anyway, and please to see me. This was what was needed. The way Peter worked at that time was to wait and see who turned up. He did not invite anyone to join. You had to show a desire or a curiosity of your own. Turning up did not guarantee a place, but it was a necessary first step.

The Space in Paris where we all spent so many hours of struggle was a large, high-ceilinged stone hall with skylights. It was empty except for a big grey-blue carpet and some strange-looking musical instruments along the side. When I arrived, Peter and some of his group had already been working for a year, travelling to Iran for a production called *Orghast*, which had been written by Ted Hughes in a made-up language. The people were unlike any I had seen before. There was Yoshi from Japan, a Kabuki actor; Miriam Goldschmidt from Germany, the beautiful result of a wartime liaison between a black American GI and a German girl; François and Sylvan, two Parisian actors, urbane and sophisticated; Michelle from the States, statuesque with a mane of red hair; and Lou Zeldis, a tall, skinny hippy with masses of blond ringlets. Lou and Michelle were former performers with La MaMa. There was also Bruce, my by now ex-boyfriend; and Malik, who combined French elegance and African roots (he came originally from Mali), a wonderful mix. We also had another American, the very Greek Andreas Katsoulas. We were to get to know each other very well.

A performance at a *bidonville* outside Paris.

We were actors not only from different races and countries, but also from different theatre disciplines. In the case of Lou and Michelle, the free-ranging, improvisational anarchy of the Living Theater and La MaMa, while Bruce and I came from the text-driven, self-controlled world of English literature and poetry, and Yoshi from the most disciplined of all, Japanese classical theatre with its intense physical and vocal demands. Sylvan and François were successful French actors with a bit of everything under their belts; likewise Andreas, whose attitude was one of terrific practicality and no pretension whatsoever.

We also had with us an American musical prodigy called Elizabeth Swados whose role was to work with us musically. She had a lot on her plate where I was concerned, for I inherited my mother's complete lack of musicality in any practical sense.

The group went by the imposing title of Le Centre International de Recherche Théâtrale, or CIRT. We started work. The intention as far as I understood it was to work towards finding a common theatrical language, or a way of communicating through theatre that owed nothing to language or any particular culture. In other words, to find a universal human theatre experience. When I say we used no language, that's not to say that we mimed. We didn't. Certainly movement was important, but so were sound and music. Again, the music could not owe anything to a particular form or culture. It was a question of throwing out everything you had learned, depended upon and built up, and trying to reconfigure it into an unrecognisable form, but one that nonetheless made a theatrical sense. It was a horribly difficult task; one that encouraged deep self-doubt and insecurity, for there seemed to be nothing to hold on to. I think all of us went through that, with the possible exception of Yoshi.

Yoshi had started work with Brook some years before. He had played Ariel in Peter's production of *The Tempest*. I had seen him in it. That had been his first experience of working in Western theatre. I think Yoshi told the story of Peter criticising him, saying 'Yoshi, Ariel is of the air, it is all lightness. Why are you stamping heavily on the ground like that?' Yoshi replied, 'I am stamping with my left foot. In Kabuki that means "Air".' It is probably an apocryphal story, but it captures the cultural difficulties we all had in acting terms. Yoshi was by this time an old hand and understood more than the rest of us. He had also had the farthest to travel. Yoshi was our foundation and the wisest of all of us by far.

Every day, under the guidance and questioning of Peter, we did exercises and improvisations designed to winkle us out of our assumptions and habits. We were asked to use our knowledge and at the same time discard it. We were asked to be ourselves in the barest, purest sense – our nationality, our tribe, our race, our psychology – and somehow translate all that into a universal context, to be simultaneously specific and general. Most of our sessions were conducted in English with some French. The Americans spoke very little French, and some of the French did not speak English. My French from my Jean Louis days was not bad, but it improved substantially as I found myself the translator for Malik. I had to translate some very esoteric and abstract ideas, so I dread to think how it came out to Malik. He showed tremendous patience. Each of us had something distinctive and different to offer, and I think that was the whole idea. We were working on a concept that would ultimately become *The Conference of the Birds*, and if we had a text at all it was that Sufi story of birds looking for a leader, or a spiritual understanding. A kind of esoteric and spiritual *Wizard of Oz*.

Every night we would repair to that great old lady of Parisian restaurants, La Coupole, which in those days was still the preferred hang-out for artists, where actors could do the things actors do: complain, gossip and laugh – although laughter was thinner on the ground than usual.

As usual, I managed to find the only hotel in town without running water. It was on Place de la Contrescarpe, then a wonderful part of the city, not known to tourists, with one of those magical food markets leading to it. I had been wandering around there and spotted this little hotel. I didn't stay longer than a couple of months, but I loved it. It was the ultimate artist's garret in Paris; a white, cell-like room with a very saggy bed and a sink in the corner with cold water only. The view from the window was the classic Parisian view of red rooftops. If you wanted a bath you had to ask Madame and pay, and she would go off and heat up some water and splosh it into a big old bath down the corridor.

At that time, the British Ambassador was a great man: Christopher Ewart Biggs. He was a classic ex-public school card-carrying member of the so-called upper classes, but also witty, very intelligent and interesting with wide-ranging interests and an open mind. He had an almost absurdly posh voice, and looked like a strange jungle bird that had taken on the form of a human. He and his wife were welcoming to starving expatriate artists and invited me to dinner in that beautiful embassy. He was later murdered by the IRA, with a car bomb. I mourned his loss.

While I was working in Paris, living the ultimate bohemian artist's life, I was asked to attend the Cannes Film Festival for the first time. *O Lucky Man!* was making its debut. I agreed, thinking it would be a nice little break by the sea for Georgie and myself (Georgie had come to Paris with me). I had no idea what I was letting myself in for. I arrived in my tattered clothes and run-down shoes, looking like a backpacker who belonged definitely and somewhat defiantly off the red carpet, behind the red rope. Amongst all those beautiful women in beautiful dresses I stuck out like a sore thumb. I remember seeing Rachel Roberts, famous for her working-class performances, swanning around like the Queen of Sheba in an enormous pink feather boa coat. The studio executives were horrified; this was not what was expected of a Warner Brothers film star. Lindsay Anderson told me off. 'You must behave more like a star, Helen, for God's sake!' It was my first taste of the pressure to look good. They gave me some money to go out and buy myself an outfit for the premiere, and a pair of shoes. We used some of it to buy Georgie a pair of shoes he had his eye on as well. White patent, I seem to remember.

In fact, George proved to be brilliant in those circumstances. He started acting like my manager and asked for a better room than the dark hole we had been given. We were duly moved to a glamorous suite, which seemed fabulously luxurious after my little garret in Paris. For a couple of days at least I had my own bathroom, all clean and new, with running hot water.

In Cannes much is made of the opening of a film. You have a big red-carpet arrival, and the photographers do their thing. I had never experienced anything like this before. I arrived at what

I thought was just a screening to find myself in front of what seemed to be thousands of cameras flashing in my face. I grabbed George's hand and ran. I didn't stop until I got to the top of the steps, where I stood shaking from top to toe, my heart beating like a drum. Nothing can prepare you for that. I have run that gauntlet many times since and it no longer makes me shake, but I still have to steel myself beforehand.

After having my inadequacies as a star exposed in Cannes, I returned to Paris and an environment where to be a star was the worst sin imaginable. Peter spoke long, articulately and disdainfully of the star system. It was the very antithesis of what we were trying to achieve with CIRT, which was the ultimate in ensemble work. At that time I was more comfortable with the ensemble scenario.

As part of our training, we studied Tai Chi (which at that time I had never heard of) and Moyshe Feldenkrais – now a legendary teacher in the world of the body, thought and posture – taught us movement. Peter was always exposing us to ideas that were profound and teachers who were brilliant.

Our work in Paris was all preparation for a further experiment: an epic journey across Africa playing through improvisation to small settlements and villages along the way. We would end the year in America, holding workshops with various theatre groups. The tour would culminate in New York, where we would perform at the Brooklyn Academy. We prepared for this journey by performing in the *bidonvilles*, the shanty-town communities of North African immigrant workers that were appearing around the outskirts of Paris. It was our first lesson in the nervous terror of this kind of performance, completely improvised and without language, although of course the fear was all in the anticipation. The reality was benign and our eccentricity was treated with humour and bemused acceptance. By this time one more performer had joined our group: the extraordinary Ayan Sola, one of the most famous performers on the 'talking drum' from the Yoruba region in Nigeria.

The day came to set off across the Sahara. We flew to Algeria, spent a few days there preparing, and then gathered our belongings to pack into the truck and Land Rovers that were to take us.

The first problem was the luggage. We had all been told in no uncertain terms to limit ourselves to one fairly small suitcase. The water situation was going to be very difficult, especially on the long trek across the Sahara. The region had been experiencing one of its many droughts, and water would be hard to come by. We were to be given one small can of water each per day for washing both our clothes and ourselves, and of course we were going to get very dirty and dusty. Most of us arrived with too much luggage, and there was much wailing and tearing of hair. Only Yoshi came prepared. His bag took up only a quarter of his luggage allowance. Later we saw why. In it he had two fine white wraps, two pairs of underwear, two white T-shirts, and two pairs of fine white cotton trousers. Every day he wore one set of clothes and washed the other. He was always immaculately clean and neat. The rest of us, for all our luggage, slowly got more and more scruffy.

We were accompanied by a group who specialised in organising 'adventure' holidays, rare at that time. They were ex-army for the most part, and saw travel through those regions as a form of military campaign. The natives were not to be mistreated, but neither should you interact with them. They undoubtedly understood more about the local geography than we did, but never understood our ways, or what we were attempting to do. I am sure the phrase 'What a load of wankers' often passed their lips. Over four months this relationship deteriorated, until finally they left us to our own devices. At that point things got better.

We travelled by day, bumping along in the Land Rovers, and made camp at night. This meant finding a spot to put your sleeping bag, digging a hole for the rubbish, making a fire, setting up the kitchen, finding wood, setting up some lighting, etc. You were on your own as far as toilet facilities were concerned; it was a small spade and the bush, the tree or the dune. We all had designated jobs. Inevitably rows erupted, mostly over people not doing their share of the washing up, and the food – it's always the food!

In between the endless days of travelling we also had to find time to rehearse, or at least to continue our exercises, both physical and mental. This was a very demanding time. Every performance was fraught with fear. Each of us had to make our own decision about going on the carpet and engaging in the performance, which was often to an audience of three women, two kids human and three kids goat. Once, though, we stumbled upon a huge Tuareg gathering. There must have been two thousand of those magnificent men in their billowing robes, as blue as the twilight sky in the desert, mounted on camels. The women were there too, milling about in their beautiful silver jewellery. We performed to this group, yelling in an effort to make something that could communicate to so many people and camels. From their superior positions on the camels' backs they regarded us with the usual bemusement and curiosity. The camels just looked bored.

The desert was freezing at night, literally, so it was hard to climb out of the warm sleeping bag as the sun rose. By 10 a.m., however, it was scorching hot. After a week or so sleeping out under the stars, I stopped using the little campbed we'd been issued with and got used to sleeping on the ground.

After dinner each night we would sit around chatting for a short while before falling exhausted to sleep. It was during this time that I struck up a friendship with the great Ayan Sola. In Paris he had been a large, lonesome enigma, shut away from us by language and culture. He must have been unbearably homesick, for he had never left his home town before. The boys in the group had befriended him somewhat and taken him out on the town, but it had been difficult for the girls to form a relationship with him. In Algeria he bought a small tape player and a recording of James Brown and every night as we penetrated the Sahara we'd listen to the sound of James Brown singing 'Git on up', over and over until we all went mad. Eventually the batteries ran out and Ayan Sola was left in silence again. No one had explained to him about the batteries. It was around this time I struck up a kind of conversation with him, that became a nightly thing. I realised that he had no idea where he was, so I drew a map in the sand and explained, and from then on we became good friends. I think we were equally lonely.

I was terribly lonely on that trip, despite living in such close circumstances with others. I did make good friends, however, with the photographer Mary Ellen Mark, who came along for some of the journey, and whose photographs are shown here. She had a marvellous way with her when she took photographs, never stealing them surreptitiously. She always asked permission, and somehow always got it, even in places where people were very frightened of and suspicious of the camera. She and Ayan Sola were the two who held me together.

So in the desert Ayan Sola and I talked, exchanging opinions and thoughts. Neither of us had any idea what the other was talking about. I would speak of whatever came into my mind and Ayan Sola would speak at length in his beautiful language, sounding exactly like his drum when he played it. The talking drum can actually speak words and phrases, hence the name. Later, when we passed through the talking drum area, I was walking on my own down a street in a small town and behind me walked a drummer, drumming out phrases. The bystanders and shoppers were convulsed with laughter. I'd love to know what he was saying without opening his mouth.

Eventually we reached the other side of the Sahara and the landscape began to turn green, and then greener. Now when we awoke it was often to find a group of curious people standing around us, at close quarters, peering down. They would look on with interest at our undignified attempts to get out of the bag modestly.

I had two favourite places in Africa, and one of these was Ayan Sola's home. There are two towns called Ife and Oshogbo, fairly close to each other; both are magical, with a deep history and culture. Ife is a holy city, considered by the Yoruba people to be the centre of the world and the birthplace of mankind, and it may well turn out to be true. The area had experienced cruel massacres, starvation and destruction in the Biafran wars not long before. The architecture here, the sense of art, of music, of painting and of sculpture was so strong. The city is also home to a complex and ancient Pantheist religion.

We travelled more or less every day in Africa, but I never tired of the travel. I liked the constant change of climate and location. Beds and chairs became unnecessary.

It was when I got to Ife and Oshogbo that I felt at home. It was also there that I lost my friend. As we crossed the border into his home territory, Ayan Sola got out of the car and did a dance of joy, speaking to himself on the drum. It was wonderful to watch, but it was clear that now Ayan Sola was home he was not going to continue on the journey.

The night in Oshogbo we said goodbye was one of our few celebrations. Some people held a party for us. In the party was someone who spoke Ayan Sola's language and mine. Ayan Sola was excited. He got hold of the interpreter and sat him down between us to translate our conversation. What then emerged was the most expressive poetic language I have ever heard, full of descriptive passages worthy of Shakespeare or Keats. It was romantic, it was utterly beautiful, mesmerising, and it completely took me by surprise. I was struck dumb. It was so beautiful I didn't want it to end. It was the last conversation I ever had with him as the next day we moved on and he stayed.

The other magical place for me was by the banks of the massive Niger River as it flows through Mali. There again I felt strangely at home, comfortable with the people and the landscape. Like all very poor people, they showed generosity and hospitality to me. I had taken by then to wandering off on my own, much happier away from the group of travellers, although of course always there for rehearsal and performance.

Our performances continued, usually sanctioned by the local chief. Once we were paid for our performance with a live goat. This set up a passionate battle between the vegetarians amongst us and the rest. It was a question of morality. Here was a village without much to eat themselves who had paid us the huge compliment of giving us something to eat. It was an insult not to eat it. The vegetarians thought we should let it go. Lou Zeldis thought we should paint it bright blue and let it go, so it could become a magical goat. Although not vegetarian, I was of the 'don't eat the goat' group. We had enough food, albeit canned and nasty, and it seemed an unnecessary taking of a little life. In the end the goat got killed and eaten with much serious ritual and ceremony. The whole thing was absurd.

A lot of our trip was absurd and ridiculous, but much was also magical and inspiring. All the

This is a typical encampment for the night. I didn't mind the physical discomfort, but I missed the sense of decoration in our living circumstances. This was compensated by the raw beauty of our surroundings.

time Peter was observing and learning, and later he was to use the experience in creating two remarkable and ground-breaking productions: *The Ik* and *Conference of the Birds*.

Finally the great African experiment was over, we reached the sea again, having travelled through Algeria, Niger, Nigeria, Dahomey (Benin), Mali, Niger again and back to Algeria. We had witnessed extraordinary things, and met with nothing but a certain restrained kindness from the people we travelled amongst. The unity of the communities we met was stronger than our own, and their example of communal living always impressive. There was undoubtedly cruelty in those societies, and suffering that we were sometimes aware of, but also a cohesion and order that was to be envied.

When I got back to London for a brief break I could no longer sleep in a bed. Beds seemed claustrophobic with their soft mattresses and pillows. I had to sleep on the floor next to the bed. I also missed the stars, having gone to sleep looking at them for four months.

Soon we were off on the second part of the year's work, which began with a workshop collaboration with El Teatro Campesino, based in San Juan Bautista, a small and lovely old Californian town with a distinct Latino heritage. It was there that I first met Taylor, now my husband, whom, however, I did not remember meeting. He was one of the observers that would turn up from time to time; Danny Valdez, who with his brother Luis had founded the theatre, was a good friend of Taylor's.

The Teatro had been formed originally as Agit-prop theatre on the picket lines and fields of the migrant agricultural workers of the San Joaquin Valley. The workers, led by the legendary Cesar Chavez, had gone on strike. Their actions had resonated all over the world, leading to a boycott against Californian grapes. The strike and boycott were still in full force and the United Farm Workers organisation was in its early days when we were working with the Teatro.

As a part of our work we travelled out into the unbearably hot and dusty valley, with mile after unending mile of vast cultivated plains. We performed on the picket lines and met Cesar Chavez, who was immediately and deeply impressive. He was quiet and gentle, sat under a tree, on a box, and spoke softly, with eloquence and simplicity, about the struggles ahead. I played the Teamsters' Contract, one of my better inventions. At that time, in order to break the strike and the Farm Workers union, a 'sweetheart contract' was being offered by the corrupt Teamsters union, an organisation then run by thugs. Happily they did not prevail, and Chavez did.

One of the greatest pleasures of our time with the Teatro was to live and work with the exuberant, unbelievably noisy Latinos that made up the group. I made some lifelong friends amongst them. It was also a terrific way to rediscover America, and its pleasures of the diner and the cocktail bar.

Our next journey was into Native American culture via the work we did with the American Indian Theater Ensemble, made up of people from various different tribes, now sadly disbanded. With them we travelled to Minnesota to work on a reservation. If you saw a photograph of where we were working it would appear very beautiful, but its beauty was overshadowed by the enormous and rampant mosquitoes that feasted on us. Living and working with these Native Americans made me appreciate the beauty inherent in their culture and society. The first night we arrived on the reservation there was no accommodation for us, so we all camped in a half-destroyed community hall. At our end of the hall, all was chaos and untidiness, and down the other end where the American Indian actors were, as soon as they unpacked it had an order and decoration that looked like home.

On the reservation there was a terrible feeling of doom and despair; we were there long before the Native Americans hit upon the brilliant scheme of building casinos that have brought wealth to neighbouring communities. The troupe themselves, although wonderful people, were also infused with a sadness, a sense of end and futility. I fell in love with one of them, a Pueblo Indian from Taos, New Mexico. We as a group were invited to attend a real pow-wow – a great honour, as it is quite rare for white people to go. A pow-wow is a big gathering for people to sing and dance and talk. There were dance competitions, and I was surprised to see my friend, Carpio, suddenly turn up in full regalia. He danced superbly, and I think he won. The pow-wow went on over three days, but as it progressed, the alcohol consumption began to rise and eventually the elders suggested that we, the foreigners, leave, as it might turn ugly for us.

I had one of the girls in the Indian troupe give me a tattoo, after a couple of brandies. She carefully and delicately wrapped cotton thread round the end of a safety pin and emptied ink out of a pen someone had. She then stabbed it into my hand. It was incredibly painful. I almost fainted and would have stopped halfway, but she forced me to go on as she knew half a tattoo would look silly. About four of us got tattooed that night.

In those days only sailors, Hell's Angels and prisoners had tattoos. In fact, it was a group of prisoners that had inspired me to get a tattoo. Whilst in France, we had performed in an old prison at Fontevraud Abbey, where Jean Genet himself had once been incarcerated. This extraordinary place, which houses the tombs of Henry II and Eleanor of Aquitaine, was once a centre for powerful women who took the veil in order to exert political influence. They advised kings and held sway in the palaces of Europe. Centuries later, I could feel those women exercising their power on me. It is a most evocative place. When we visited it was in the process of being changed from prison to renovated cultural site, and we performed to the few prisoners left. They were all tattooed with eye make-up or tears. A combination of the memory of those prisoners and the powerful atmosphere of Fontevraud made me want to commemorate it, which I did in Minnesota with my tattoo.

After the reservation we went on to New York, the final leg of the journey as far as I was concerned. We performed the most rehearsed of our performances and held workshops at the Brooklyn Academy. We were still improvising, but in a more rehearsed way. Performances never lost their terror, however. We also continued our tradition of street theatre by performing in deepest Brooklyn for various ethnic groups. The most frightening of these by far were the Italian-Americans, who were much more aggressive than the African Americans. There was almost a riot when we performed in a park in an Italian neighbourhood. The bamboo sticks we used as props to create a spiritual experience were used to poke us unmercifully, and in the end we had to run for it, with the mob howling after us.

At the end of this, one of the best years of my life, and also one of the most difficult, I decided that I wanted to return to the more normal life of an actor. I especially missed the use of language, and the ease of performing in your own language to people who understand you. I also felt I would never be frightened of anything ever again. Unfortunately that was not the case. And so I bade farewell to my friends. The following year I saw many of them performing in the production Peter mounted called *Conference of the Birds*. It was one of the best things I have ever seen in the theatre.

Here is the company of international actors
working in Paris. We sat for hour after hour
cross-legged around a blue-grey carpet. Peter
Brook was indefatigable. He was also inspiring,
articulate, profoundly intelligent and somewhat
intimidating.

Left, middle right:
The legendary Moyshe
Feldenkrais with whom
we directly worked.

Bottom right: Miriam
Goldschmidt, Irene Brook
and me. Irene and I
are trying to be as cool
and exotic as Miriam.

Below: My friend to this day, the superb photographer Mary Ellen Mark, who accompanied us through much of Africa. She took all these pictures.
Right: Lou Zeldis and I enjoy the sea, having travelled across Africa to reach it.
Below right: We exercise in the desert. So very serious.
Opposite: The cold desert mornings.

CHARLIE MIRIAM. PETER FRACIS BOB APPLE
MAGGIE MAURICE RICHARD LIZ
MAY

HANAY MARY IRENE.
TIFFANY YOSHI HELEN
CARPIO

AS P.WICCON        M.ANTONETTE NINA
MELE          MALIK.        BRUCE  NANCY

LD PHILS  PHIL  NATASHA               ANDY
FRIEND                    JANE  JOHN
INA           SIMON              VACCARRO.

Previous pages:
The group in Northern
Minnesota, on an Indian
reservation and working with
the American Indian Theater
Ensemble, now sadly disbanded.
Opposite: Some of our
performances in Africa, and
one of our encampments. We
travelled every day, and made
camp each night.

With Carpio, I am in love.

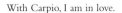

Carpio surprised me
at the pow-wow in
Minnesota by suddenly
appearing in his dancing costume and
dancing with bravura. No wonder I fell in
love. He was a Pueblo Indian from Taos,
New Mexico. The city life was not for him,
and soon after our work together he went
home to Taos, where his heart was.

Limekiln Creek Bridge, near Big Sur on scenic
Highway 1 along California's magnificent coastline. The Santa Lucia mountain range dominates
the inland scenery. The limekilns after which the
creek is named were brought in by ship in the
1880's and can be visited by hikers.

This place is even more
beautiful than shown on the
card. I drove there for my
day off (only 1½ hrs drive
from here) in my red convertible
Pontiac I have bought (to
sell when I leave). We have
also spent a lot of time
working for the Huelga (strike)
It has become very serious because
the growers want to take away
all improvements made in life and
dignity of farm workers. So life goes on
in its usual insane and beautiful way. love Pop xxxx

C19822—Color Photo by Randy Larson

MR & MRS MIRREN
20 QUEENS ROAD
LEIGH-ON-SEA
ESSEX.
ENGLAND

P.S. It lovely to get
a letter and 2

I tried to keep in touch with family and
friends while travelling but found it impossible
to describe what we were really experiencing. It
was easier to be polite or silly.

A letter to my friends
Sandy and Lindy, who
were staying at my
house while I was away.

A Local HAT: →

Dear Sand Lind and all.
Through the Jungle and at the
other side we are now clawing our
way back up the map Machetes
flying Mosquitoes biting regularly
running out of water and getting
malaria. I'm sitting on a tree trunk
under a Mango Tree in the morning
warmth before it gets so hot all
you can do is sit sweating and
gasping in the shade wishing for cool
water and ice tinkling in glasses
instead of _hot_ sterilized $H_2O$ from
a little portable pump. We are by the
Niger wich is cool enough but you are
supposed to get HORRIBLE diseases
from it like maggots that get into
your _bones_ and _EAT_ them from the
INSIDE AAAArrrggghhh. They
get in through the sales of your
feet. O well. If I suddenly fall
down and cant get up again when

The flat in Doria Road, Fulham.

When I got back, the culture shock was quite
extreme. Even on the plane coming home the waste
seemed terrible. I had spent exactly one year
with the CIRT. It was frustrating, enlightening,

confusing and stimulating, but I wanted to get back
to my country and try to put some of what I
had learned into my work in mainstream theatre.
I was also quite happy to be wearing gold shoes again.

# Theatre

*My life on the stage – Lady Macbeth to Natalya Petrovna*

**The first production** I appeared in after leaving the CIRT in New York was *Macbeth*, in Stratford, directed by Trevor Nunn, with Nicol Williamson playing the man himself. This was a case where the actor was so suited for the role that it overwhelmed him. He could not rehearse it.

Days were spent waiting for Nicol to get going. He would argue terribly with Trevor and was just horrible to me. I think his plan, if there was such a thing, was to hold back until the first night and then just let it explode. This meant there was no organisation to the performance and it went far too fast, leaving nowhere to go after about the third scene. Coming from the ensemble experience of Brook, I was thrown right into the deep end of a pool where ego and self-centredness were paramount. It certainly had a kind of power, but was an absolutely miserable experience. The production was also very designed. Having come from a year of making theatre with just a carpet I balked at being a cog in a design.

I wrote a letter to the *Guardian*, saying that I thought subsidised theatre was becoming too concerned with design issues and losing the art of acting. The powers that be at the RSC were horrified. I understood. To maintain the subsidy was always a struggle, so my letter did not help. However I was also treated with condescension.

Three years later Trevor did the production I'd been dreaming of, with no set, in an empty space and simple costumes and it was one of his biggest successes.

By then I think I had really begun my life as a professional actress. Although the process of learning has never stopped for me, at that point my apprenticeship had ended and the real work began.

Soon after *Macbeth*, which played both at Stratford and in London, I was asked by Lindsay Anderson to do a season in the West End appearing in a couple of plays in repertoire at the Lyric: Chekhov's *The Seagull* and *The Bed Before Yesterday* by the inimitable, the glorious Ben Travers. I liked the idea of the contradiction in the choice of these two plays, and I could work again with the iconoclastic, acerbic and loyal Lindsay Anderson, with whom I had done *O Lucky Man!*.

I had a funny relationship with Lindsay. We seemed to be old friends from the moment we met, able to tease one another and loving each other, or at least I loved him. He had this effect on many people and I felt privileged to be accepted by him.

Ben Travers was also a memorable man. He had been a wildly successful West End playwright in the thirties and forties, writing perfectly constructed farces that are now classics. Now in his eighties, he had written a marvellous new farce. It was typical of Lindsay to want to direct the play, as Lindsay had no ability to follow fashion, having instead a simple dedication to everything he thought was good.

Ben was full of laughter and sparkle. He wore his age like a very thin disguise over a sexy, alert and utterly humane persona. I adored him. For his eighty-ninth birthday I gave him a silly T-shirt with something written on the front like I'm sexy, and he put it on under his straight suit.

I believe it is only by performing in a play eight times a week that you really understand its strengths and weaknesses. A critic, coming to a play on the first night, really cannot fathom the totality of it; often they are bamboozled by sets, directing, acting even. Ben's play, like all his others, was a marvel of construction and wit. My part was nothing to write home about, the usual girly role, but I was happy to serve the play as best I could. In fact, although I was often cast in those roles, I was pretty hopeless at them. Something inside me would be at war with the character, so I was always overcomplicating the part.

The season had been constructed around Joan Plowright. Joan was playing Arkadina in *The Seagull*, and I was Nina. I had heard it was a good role, but I hadn't actually read the play when we started rehearsals. I always find plays and scripts very difficult to read; I can never understand who is who or where they are supposed to be. Besides, I am terminally lazy.

As Nina in *The Seagull*, 1975.

Lindsay thought we should spend a week reading and deconstructing the play before rehearsals began, so we met in Joan's lovely London flat. We read the first act, and discussed it at length. We read the second act and discussed it. During that discussion I said innocently, 'Gosh, I wonder if Nina and Tregorin have an affair.' Joan turned her blackberry eyes in horror upon me. 'Have you read the play, Helen?' Consummate professional that she was, and married to the greatest living actor, she must have thought that the younger generation was going to the dogs. She had a point.

Joan also played Alma, the lead in the Ben Travers play. The male lead was another great professional actor, John Moffat. John was kind and funny. Joan and he earned my undying respect one night when the edge of the curtain, as it rose, caught the tablecloth on a table right downstage and sent a complete tea service crashing to the floor. The scene they were about to perform, a very elegant tea party drenched with sexual innuendo, was played by Joan and John on their hands and knees, fetching sugar lumps, sandwiches, saucers, milk jugs and teapots from all over the stage. Their aplomb brought the house down.

When I look back at the amount of work I did in this period I am surprised that I managed to fit it all in. I returned to the RSC to play Margaret in *Henry VI* and finally felt the power to fill that theatre. I also played a number of leading roles in television dramas: in 1974 there was the seventeenth-century play *Bellamira*, a thriller, *Coffin for the Bride*, and another wonderful Jacobean play, *The Changeling*; in 1975 I did *Caesar and Claretta*, the story of Mussolini and Claretta Petacci, followed by *The Philanthropist* by Christopher Hampton, *The Little Minister* by J. M. Barrie, and *The Apple Cart* by Shaw. In that same year I appeared in David Hare's *Teeth 'n' Smiles*; it first played at the Royal Court and then transferred to the West End in 1976.

That year I also did *The Collection* by Pinter on television with Laurence Olivier, Alan Bates and Malcolm McDowell. It was an amazing time for television drama. In 1977 I did Wycherley's *The Country Wife*, in 1978 *As You Like It* playing Rosalind, and in 1979 *Blue Remembered Hills* by Dennis Potter.

And that was also the year I spent four months in Rome shooting *Caligula*. And at the beginning of this period, I met and fell in love with the photographer James Wedge.

My first
production
after I came
back was with
the RSC again,
playing Lady
Macbeth to
Nicol Williamson's Macbeth in 1975.
This play is supposed to be
cursed Thank God nothing
disastrous happened in our
production except in the
relationship between Nicol
and me. He hated me.

1945

# Stage set for an empty pageant?

*Helen Mirren*

Sir,—There has been much made of the quaking economics of the Royal Shakespeare Company and the National Theatre by the culturally-conscious press; with the exception of Michael Billington's remarkable review of Timon of Athens in Paris, little is made of the quaking artistry of those companies in particular.

To myself and many colleagues of my generation who have been involved in work with the National and the R.S.C. the expenditure on costumes sets and staging in general has been excessive, unnecessary and destructive to the art of Theatre.

The English Theatre has been admired by Europe and the West for the quality of its acting and direction, not for the richness of its decoration. But those two elusive and delicate ingredients are the ones that are becoming obliterated in music cues, lighting cues, computerised scene shifting, real silk, real leather—a pageant fit for a king but not much else.

A piece of theatre needs a space, an audience, some actors, a lot of imagination, a leader and if a play, a great one. All those are available to the subsidised companies, plus a lot of money. Of course the big companies have a duty to their audiences to produce big and fulfilling productions, but the realms of truth, emotion and imagination reached for in the acting of a great play have become more and more remote, often totally unreachable across an abyss of costume and technicalities.

The only way to protect yourself and your performance from obliteration is to return to that old-fashioned style of withdrawing from all about you and acting in a vacuum, which, if you are not among the world's greatest actors, leads to selfishness and hysteria.

Our importance in these economy-obsessed days is recognised by how much we cost and an actor has become the cheapest thing on the stage.

Theatre moves slowly, eroding or evolving as a reflection of or a guidance to the world about it. With of course the exception of regional theatre, I feel the need for economy demanded at this moment could be the saving of our theatre. — Yours sincerely,

**Helen Lydia Mirren.**
Stretton-in-Fosse,
Moreton-in-Marsh,
Gloucestershire.

utter or a motorist's

**Funding faith**

This is the letter I sent to the 'Guardian', complaining about excessive sets and designs. I was fresh from Brook's concept of 'An Empty Space'. This letter led to a question in Parliament. I was condescendingly and sexistly described as complaining about a few yards of tulle.

The Lyric Theatre

*The Sea Gull*

by

*ANTON CHEKHOV*

In *The Seagull* and
Ben Travers' *The Bed
Before Yesterday*, both
in 1975.

Working with Lindsay Anderson and Joan Plowright in a West End
repertory season of 'The Seagull' and 'Bed before Yesterday' was a
memorable experience. The stage door of the Lyric Theatre is right
next to the Windmill Theatre, just off Shaftesbury Avenue. I got
to know the call girls and their pimps who hung out there. They
were very friendly and sweet, the girls in particular. I loved being
one of the Windmill Street crowd. On some Saturday nights the
sounds of a very drunken football hooligan crowd would penetrate
the walls of the theatre and I would play the final scene of the
Chekhov, Nina's famous, heartbreaking 'I am a seagull' speech, to
the not so distant sounds of 'AAAARRRSSSENAAAAALLL'
and the inevitable police siren following on.

### It's only rock'n'roll

I was doing *Teeth 'n' Smiles*, which for the first time brought the world of rock and roll into the theatre. My dressing room overlooked the back alley. One Friday night, waiting for my last entrance, I heard the most almighty crashing about coming from the alley. I looked out of the window and saw a man in a pinstriped suit who had fallen into the dustbins and was rolling around on the ground with the rubbish. A drunk. Then I heard the kerfuffle – shouting down the stairwell in the vicinity of the stage door, which then came up the stairs and stopped right outside my dressing room. I opened the door and there was the man in the suit – Keith Moon, legendary drummer of The Who – with the stage door man hovering anxiously behind. He staggered into my dressing room and very sweetly said 'Hi' and how great he'd heard the show was. I was thrilled to meet him, but just then the call for my last entrance came over the tannoy. I said I was sorry but I had to go on stage. He said not to worry – he'd come with me! I tried to dissuade him, but he assured me he was used to being on stage. He then followed me down the stairs to the wings where, sadly, he was stopped by the management. I have always regretted that I was too much of an actor that night and not rock and roll enough to have insisted on the once-in-a-lifetime opportunity to be on stage with a legend like K. Moon, albeit drunk and out of his mind.

My second and best
go at Cleopatra, in the
small theatre with the
RSC, 1982. This was
brilliantly directed by
Adrian Noble. Here
I am with my friend
Sorcha Cusack as
Charmian.

*The Duchess of Malfi*
with Bob Hoskins at
the Roundhouse, 1980.

The Royal Exchange Theatre
at the Round House

The Duchess of Malfi

*by John Webster*

Sorcha was also in the magnificent production of 'The Duchess of Malfi', also directed by Adrian. Here I am having a costume fitting. I would say that the three greatest productions I have been in were 'Duchess of Malfi', 'Orpheus Descending', directed by Nick Hytner, and 'Mourning Becomes Electra', directed by Howard Davies. It is no coincidence that all three were designed by Bob Crowley, now the best and most sought-after designer working in the theatre. Contrary to what I wrote to the 'Guardian', great design in the theatre can be the element that elevates it to something legendary. I love to see design that does not fight with the material or performers but informs and frames the production in an astounding and imaginative way. As an actress, there is nothing like being on a marvellous set to present your play. It is not a question of sheer beauty. When the set, the lighting and the costumes combine together to both surprise and delight the audience, it smooths your way. It makes the whole such a pleasure to be a part of. Bob's designs do this.

Here is my third Cleopatra, this time with Alan Rickman.
This was a big and ornamental production in the Olivier Theatre at
the National. It was a failure, but I loved playing the serpent of
old Nile again, especially in that operatic space. You cannot perform
Shakespeare's plays too often. Each time you can find something new
in every line. Also you have the great advantage of knowing the lines.
When I played it the second time with Michael Gambon as Antony,
on the second day's rehearsal I found I knew the whole play, from
playing it for one week all those years before in the Youth Theatre.
Lovely, because I loathe learning lines.

Ruby Wax, an old friend from my Brad Davis years in America so long before, visited me backstage after the first night. She came crowned as the Queen of Thailand. She swore she'd worn it throughout the performance. I had to put my crown back on just to compete.

Rehearsing for 'Two-Way Mirror' at the Young Vic,
the writer visited us, the great man himself, Arthur
Miller. He spent a week with us. Like all the great
people I have met he was at the same time deeply
intelligent but simple, impressive but approachable.
His greatest quality was his absolute love of and
dedication to his craft and his chosen art form,
the theatre.

'Mourning Becomes Electra' gave me one of the greatest roles for a woman. Christine Mannon and I knew nothing about it before coming to it. This production was one of the best experiences of my professional life. The play was four and a half hours long, and I have never known that kind of response from an audience. People would be literally shaking at the end. It was the serendipity of a beautifully cast play, with great design and direction. It will be hard to be in anything better.

## New York, 9/11 2001

In 2001 I was asked to do Strindberg's *Dance of Death* on Broadway with Ian McKellen. We began rehearsals in the thick heat of a New York August. On September 11, I was up at 7.30 a.m. to go from my rented apartment in Chelsea to our rehearsal room for a last run-through of the play before moving into the theatre. My husband was in London, overseeing the renovations of our London house. At 8.35 a.m. he rang me to discuss what sort of taps (faucets to the Americans) we should have in the bathroom. My sister was with him, talking to her son, Simon, on her mobile. He was on the Internet at the time, and suddenly said to her that a plane had flown into the World Trade Center. It was 8.45 a.m. When Taylor told me, I turned on the television to see the morning news, but there was no mention of it. I told Taylor and we agreed that it was Simon being dramatic.

Then it suddenly came on. At this point it was not clear that this was no accident. And then the second plane hit. I watched in horror, and incomprehension. Just before 10 a.m. a car arrived to take me to the rehearsals. As we drove to Times Square, I saw people on the street stop and look with an indescribable expression downtown. I looked back and saw that horrible slow-motion collapse of the first building.

Not knowing what else to do, we continued to the rehearsal rooms. When we arrived, some of our cast who had friends downtown had to leave to see what they could do. Ian and I decided to simply go ahead as planned, and we had a strange but somehow comforting run-through of that darkly funny play. In the breaks I went outside. Above the entrance to the building we were working in was one of those huge Times Square screens, and it was showing all the horrors coming out of the downtown district. People, not knowing what else to do, were standing across the road, looking up at this screen in silence, that indescribable wondering and slightly blank look of disbelief and horror etched on their faces.

All the businesses in the area were now closed, all that is bar one. When I went out looking for some food for lunch, the only business still open was a video porn show, and I saw someone going in. I can't make up my mind if that was wonderful or terrible.

The screen at Times Square, showing events unfolding.

In the following weeks I learned to respect the New Yorkers for their great courage and resilience. I had always wondered, as a post-Second World War child whose parents had experienced the Blitz, what the ethnically diverse and culturally conflicted people of the great American cities would do if they had bombs dropped on them the way Londoners and the people of Coventry did. I had thought that they would split into factions, at each other's throats. How wrong I was. They came together – Puerto Ricans, Ukrainians, Blacks, Jews, Indians, Italians, Chinese and all the great mix that is New York – and became one homogenous city in their grief, rising to the challenge. It was a terrible time of vast tragedy and I think it changed New York for ever. It became a stronger place, a better place in its heart. They were incredible, and I was very content to be there amongst them. And yes, they even came to the theatre.

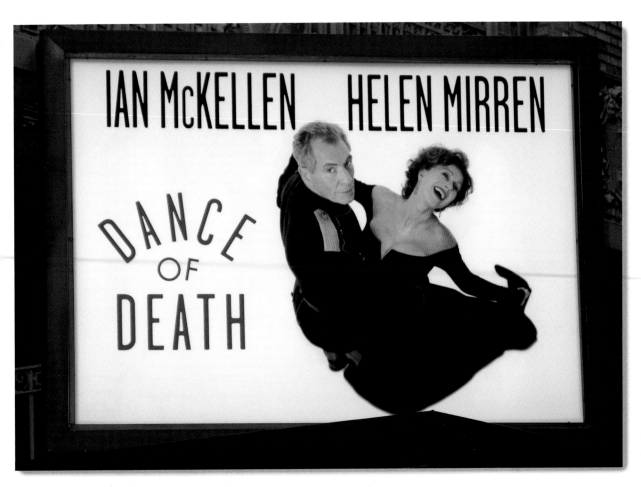

### A bad case of the giggles

I did *A Month in the Country* twice, once in London and again in New York with a different director and cast. Both productions were very successful. I loved this play and the part of Natalya Petrovna. It was in New York that my friend and co-actor Ron Rifkin got such a bad case of the giggles that he walked off stage during a scene between the two of us and I suddenly found myself all alone on stage. I walked up and down a bit, trying to think of a soliloquy that would cover the necessary ground for the play to make sense. Ron then suddenly appeared in the doorway, red in the face, opened his mouth to speak, squeaked, and then turned around and walked off again. Luckily in a few seconds he had managed to compose himself and we played the love scene with me shooting dark looks at him.

Jennifer Garner was the understudy for the young girl. She would stand in the wings to watch. She was the loveliest young girl, both inside and out, and still is. No one could deserve the success she has had more.

During the run I got caught by a hurricane in New Orleans. The airport closed, and no cabs worked. I skidded into the theatre with five minutes to spare, having fought tooth and nail all day to get there. It was my finest hour.

WINNER

OUTER CRITICS CIRCLE AWARD · OUTSTANDING DEBUT OF AN ACTRESS

HELEN MIRREN

3 DRAMA DESK AWARD NOMINATIONS
INCLUDING
HELEN MIRREN OUTSTANDING ACTRESS IN A PLAY

"A Month in the Country
is an enthralling, deeply entertaining
production. Helen Mirren is riveting"
— Howard Kissel, Daily News

"Intoxicating. Ron Rifkin is especially touching."
— Linda Winer, Newsday

"F. Murray Abraham is fascinating to watch."
— Robert Feldberg, The Record

"It is a joy to see this wonderful play so movingly and delightfully realized.
Scott Ellis does his best work yet – he shines."
— Donald Lyons, The Wall Street Journal

"Helen Mirren makes a triumphant Broadway debut."
— Clive Barnes, New York Post

"A gutsy, smart and sexy star,
this is Helen Mirren's Broadway
debut and it's about time"
— Jack Kroll, Newsweek

"A superb ensemble cast."
— Robert Osborne, The Hollywood Reporter

"The bewitching
Helen M
— Liz Sm

THIS PRODUCTION SPONSORED BY THE
Roundabout Theatre
1530 BROADWAY AT 45TH STREET

A MONTH IN THE COUNTRY

ALBERY THEATRE

## Dressing rooms

Dressing rooms are an important part of backstage life, be they scruffy and cramped or spacious and decorated. It does not really matter either way. It's nice to have somewhere to lie down between shows (at the Donmar I had to lie down in the broom cupboard), but otherwise all you need is a sink, a mirror above a table, and some light. I usually decorate my room, if I am on my own, with a special antique Chinese rug I have, some fairy lights, and a couple of cushions. I also have a leather-covered make-up box that was one of the gifts left behind by my glamorous Auntie Olga all those years ago in Southend. The box was originally a case of Elizabeth Arden products. It is now very funky and grubby, but I love it and always have it with me in the theatre. It has been through every production I have ever done, starting with the Youth Theatre.

For the duration of the play, the dressing room becomes your domain, your territory. You experience exultation and despair in that room, a beating heart and sweaty hands, and you never want to leave it and you dread entering it. It becomes an intrinsic part of your existence, more familiar than your home. Then the play finishes and you have to leave it for the next actor. From the moment you turn in the key to the stage door keeper that room has absolutely no more meaning for you. It becomes an empty vessel waiting for the next actor and his or her make-up box and fears, excitement, jubilation and anguish.

We did 'Orpheus' at the Donmar with one tiny dressing room shared between all the women. There were about eight of us. I loved it. Every night we would take turns at buying a bottle of champagne to share at the end of the show. We would then stick the corks on a shelf above the mirrors. I wonder if they are still there.

# James Wedge

*Extraordinary photographs by an extraordinary artist*

**James, when I met him**, was a successful fashion and beauty photographer, one of the wave of London-born photographers of the late sixties and early seventies, the era of David Bailey, Donovan, the King's Road and all that.

'Swinging sixties' London had completely passed me by. I guess I was working too intensely and was too obsessed with theatre to notice anything else. Besides, whenever I found myself anywhere near the King's Road it seemed to me that I had stumbled into a club I most certainly did not belong to and where all the other members thought I should be ejected ASAP. The girls were thin and long-legged with expensive clothes and the blokes looked superior and arrogant. It was an intimidating environment, especially when, like me, you were found wanting. It had changed from the artists' hang-out of my father's time to the protected territory of the über-fashionistas.

James had been a part of that world, and still was to a certain extent. He had for some of the sixties been the most famous milliner in London, and then had run a very successful King's Road boutique before turning to 'smudging' – the old East End term for photography, for he was a truly working-class boy, born in Hoxton back when it was the epicentre of the East End and not the trendy spot it is now. He was and is self-educated, brilliant, funny and very artistic. Just in time to catch the last years of National Service, he had joined the navy; his tales of being on a ship bound for Australia to carry out the first British atomic blasts made me cry with laughter. His photography was gorgeous, and to me a new revelation of art.

I have always loved the visual arts, and having missed out on my teenage dream of going to art school I learned a lot from James. He taught me about different photographers and their work: Bill Brandt, Ansel Adams, Man Ray, Brassaï, Diane Arbus, Helmut Newton. He taught me about

James and his dog Tom.

printing, how to burn and dodge and solarise. He taught me about aperture and shutter speed. At that time, James was the first photographer to resurrect the old art of hand painting on photography, and produced some very beautiful pieces. He taught me how to do that too.

His work was full of imagination and often ahead of its time. I remember him fighting to use a black model for a cover shoot, and coming up against stiff resistance. He was horrified by the unspoken racism of the fashion magazines, who refused to use black models on their covers at that time.

He and I worked together on photo shoots that were nothing to do with publicity or fashion. They were our own private pictures. Being purely visual, this work was the perfect antidote to the work I was doing in the theatre.

Another antidote was James's cottage in the Forest of Dean. There, not too far from where my mother had

been evacuated to all those years before, I could continue the enjoyment of the countryside that had begun for me in Stratford.

The Forest of Dean is a very particular place, a strange and individual landscape that combines rural and industrial. Poor but self-sufficient, it was free of that side of British country life that I don't enjoy: the landowners and huge estates, the huntin', shootin' and fishin' crowd. There is no cap-doffing in the Forest of Dean. Originally a royal hunting forest favoured by kings and queens since Norman times, it never became agricultural land where farmworkers laboured for the benefit of landowners. There are coal and iron ore mines in the area, but even these were worked by 'freeminers' who, having been born there, had the right to mine on an individual basis rather than as slave labour for wealthy mine owners. The people there are independent and proud, exercising ancient rights to look after the forest and its animals. The only people who are allowed to run sheep are those who were born in the forest. The sheep run free, marked by the farmers with different colours so people know to whom they belong. Our neighbours, Mr and Mrs Braine, were sheep farmers and smallholders with an encyclopaedic knowledge of country matters and anything horticultural, especially the growing of vegetables.

James, the archetypal city boy, must have had rural roots for he loved the countryside and its ways. He was a superb gardener and dry-stone wall builder. He taught me about both. I had never gardened before, and soon became obsessed, reading all I could get my hands on. I still like to go to bed with a gardening book, reading up on the best soil for amaryllis, how to grow peonies and what insects attack broccoli.

Those days with James I count as some of the happiest in my life. On Saturday night he would pick me up from the theatre at 11 p.m. after the second show had finished and we would set off on the two and a half hour drive to the forest. By 1.30 a.m. we would be out in the garden, checking to see if the carrots had grown yet. Then we would work all day Sunday, and as much of Monday as possible – back-breaking hard labour, double-trenching the potatoes and so forth – before setting off to arrive in time for the evening performance. I still miss that cottage and that part of the world.

Theses pictures were for a fashion magazine.
They were shot in a beautiful old derelict music
hall theatre in the middle of Hoxton, where
James was born. The photographs were taken in
black and white, then hand-coloured by James.
I worked on the shoot as model and
photographer's assistant.

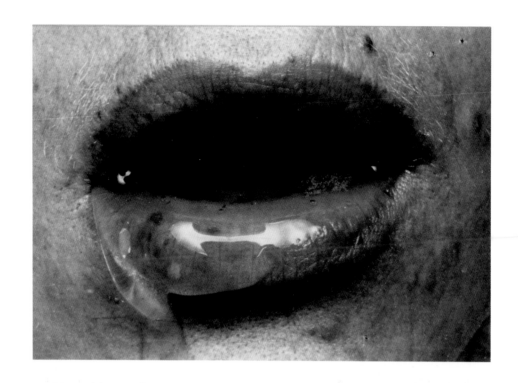

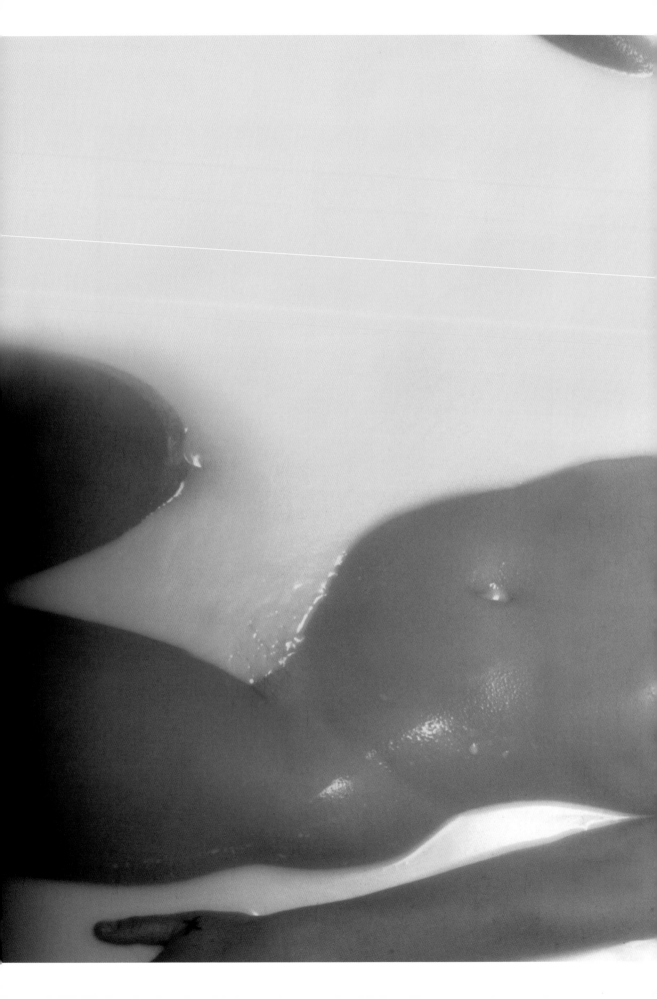

Previous pages: These
pictures were taken in
some rented apartment
while I was working.

James took some
production shots of
'The Duchess of Malfi'.
Although that was not his
speciality, they are better
than any others.

# In Front of the Camera

*From the East End to Northern Ireland*

*The Long Good Friday* came to me in the usual way, a script sent via my agent, but what a script! Barrie Keeffe wrote for the theatre and this script read like a piece of literature, full of life and wonderful dialogue. It was the best film script I had ever read. It had been written with Bob Hoskins in mind and was a perfect role for him, playing right to the strengths of his energy. I don't think I was who they had in mind for the role of Victoria, however. The character was somewhat insipid and predictable, a cipher really, just the sidekick bimbo – a typical female character in the movies at that time, or maybe at any time. Nevertheless I was interested, partly because there were no great films being made in Britain at that time, and this was at least different and well written (apart from the woman).

When I met with Barrie and John Mackenzie, the director, I told them of my concerns about the character. They listened and between us we came up with some suggestions as to how Victoria might be brought further into the story. About four days before I was due to start work the new script arrived. As far as I could tell, nothing had been changed. I was devastated. I wanted to pull out, unable to bear the thought of playing this shadow of a person. However, that was contractually impossible, so I decided to speak my mind.

From that moment on I must have been such a pain to John. Every day that I worked, and sometimes even when I didn't, I would arrive with script-change ideas that would make Victoria more proactive and more central to the story. Bob Hoskins was very bighearted throughout this sometimes difficult process, which was typical of Bob, as anyone who knows him will recognise. He was playing Harold with all the fury and terrifying suppressed energy that he could. It was a very demanding role. I admire him and will be for ever grateful to him for having the generosity to be aware and supportive of my efforts. Without him, I was lost. Sometimes we would improvise a scene; sometimes I would have scribbled it down on a ratty piece of paper. At the time I had no idea whether all this was working or not.

I think John must have come to dread the scenes that involved me, wanting simply to get on and shoot the thing. You are under such intense pressure as a director, a pressure that now I understand, being married to one. The weather, the budget, the studio … To have to deal with an annoyingly opinionated actress rewriting the script whenever she came on set must have been very frustrating.

Shoot it he did, making a really great film, full of the energy of the script and his own talent for raw and visceral film-making. Much of it was shot in undeveloped, still bomb-shattered parts of Wapping. The film was prescient in its understanding of what was to come. The Margaret Thatcher years had just begun, and the East End was ripe for developers. I was blown away when I finally saw the piece. John's work was terrific, Bob's performance legendary, and I was happy to see that all the struggles to bring Victoria to life had paid off. She was now at least an intrinsic part of the story.

I have made three of my most important films in Ireland, and along the way had a wonderful relationship with an Irishman, Liam Neeson. I met Liam on the first of these films, *Excalibur*, made by the iconoclast John Boorman. John bravely cast very green actors in his film. Green but talented, as we now see, with Liam, Gabriel Byrne and Cherie Lunghi in the cast. He wanted to shoot the film in his beloved Wicklow, and I had the good fortune to spend some time in Dublin. In the process I fell in love both with Liam and with Ireland.

Liam was from Northern Ireland, having grown up Catholic in a very Protestant town, Ballymena, the home town of that war-mongering priest, Ian Paisley. He introduced me to his family: his mother, father and sisters. On that day I felt as if I were going to my execution. I was terrified of meeting them. I was so wrong for Liam, in every way: I was British, I was irreligious, and I was older than him. He had grown up the only son in a family of girls, but not at all spoilt, and it made him into the kind of man he is, completely relaxed and understanding of women, the kind of man who can look a woman directly in the eye – a quality rarer than one might imagine. I think that men who grow up with sisters are

Me and Liam Neeson.

wiser about women than others. His family was welcoming and gracious, and I became close to them.

Before starting *Excalibur*, I expressed my discomfort to John Boorman about working with Nicol Williamson again after the miserable experience of *Macbeth*. Nicol had been cast as Merlin and I was to play Morgana; we had all of our scenes together. Oddly enough, on my way to meet with John to talk about the film, my taxi was held up in traffic and I caught sight of Nicol in the back of a car in the next lane. Telling myself, Oh well, let bygones be bygones, I might as well be sociable, I waved. And got a dead-fish look in response. Hurriedly, I looked away, only to find myself staring at a street sign: Macbeth Street. Needless to say, I arrived full of doom, believing it would never work out.

John sensibly ignored all signs of disaster and cast us both anyway. In fact, Nicol became a good friend to me on this film. I was just becoming entangled with Liam and was feeling miserable about it, mainly because of the age difference. One day, as the two of us sat alone in the make-up trailer, Nicol turned to me and in that distinctive nasal drawl asked, 'So what's the matter with you then?' He listened as I blurted out my predicament, then said, 'Don't worry, it probably wouldn't work out if you were eight years younger than him either, so you may as well go for it.' Words of pessimistic wisdom that I have often thought about, or at least the 'Don't worry, just go for it' part anyway. Nicol is a difficult, inspired, brilliant, vulnerable person and on *Excalibur* I grew to care a lot for him.

With Liam I visited the North of Ireland often and saw the great beauty of the place. I also saw the difficulties related to the British occupation. Going into a shop your bag would be searched, and the police stations looked like concentration camps, covered in razor-wire and with lookout posts. Tanks rolling down the road were an everyday occurrence, and walking home one night from a restaurant, Liam and I were shadowed by an armed soldier, either protecting us or suspicious of us, you never knew. These were the very darkest days of sectarian killings. Many issues that were then common knowledge amongst the local people are only now coming to light, such as the collusion between the British forces, the RUC and the illegal Loyalist military organisations.

However, the most surprising element of that whole scenario was the terrific sense of humour that the people of Northern Ireland, whether Catholic or Protestant, shared. They laughed a lot and were very funny to be with. 'Good craic', as they call it in Ireland, is important, and we'd spent many nights in Dublin bars enjoying the craic, but I did not expect to find it in Belfast or Ballymena at that time. If anything, the sense of humour in the North was sharper than in the South. As with anywhere, people are kind, friendly and fun when you get them away from their ideologies – or maybe because of them, who knows?

My relationship with Liam and the time we'd spent in the North led me into two more Irish films, both with the Troubles as their background, and both trying to give a human face to a struggle that had demonised both sides, in the time-honoured way of war. The first of these was *Cal*, a love story that crossed both the age and the religious line. And then, much later, *Some Mother's Son*, about a hunger striker and his family.

Produced by Jim Sheridan and written and directed by Terry George, the latter was an attempt to present a viewpoint that was apolitical and anti rhetoric, showing a human conflict within a family against the backdrop of struggle and hatred. The film was planned and executed during the peace process of 1994, when it seemed that peace would be at last possible in the North. I would not have contemplated doing that film a few years earlier. By the time the film was finished, however, we were back to the times of suspicion, bias and bigotry, with the peace process destroyed by two acts of terrorism: the bomb that went off in Canary Wharf and then, later that year, the outrage and cowardly cruelty that was the bombing of Manchester city centre. I was in Manchester at the time, filming *Prime Suspect*. We were on location in a morgue, of all places, and heard both the bomb in the distance and then the endless wail of the ambulance sirens.

I think the Los Angeles-based producers and financiers of the film, Castlerock, had no idea what a potentially hot potato this film might be in Britain and Ireland. They saw it in a balanced and unprejudiced way for what it was, the story of a family. The very title shows where the heart of the film lies: every soldier, no matter what side they are on, is 'Some Mother's Son'. However, in the light of the atrocities committed by the IRA, some needed to perceive it as a pro-Republican film. This made the release difficult and I had some sticky moments promoting it. The worst of these was when, after I had been persuaded to appear on the *Today* programme, the interviewer started off by saying, 'So why did you make a film that condones acts of terrorism?' My mouth went dry. She hadn't seen the film, of course. It was the first time I had personally experienced the battle between creativity and the accepted political posture of the moment.

Opposite: Playing Beaty Simons
in *Hussy*, 1980.
Above: I took this photograph of
the border while filming in Ireland.
Left: *Some Mother's Son* 1996.
Below: With John Lynch in *Cal*,
1984.

Left: With Malcolm
McDowell in
*O Lucky Man!*, 1973.
Below right: With
Scott Antony
in *Savage Messiah*,
1972.
Below left and
bottom: With Bob
Hoskins in *The
Long Good Friday*.
Opposite: During
a break in filming
*Caligula*, Rome,
1980.

Having worked with Malcolm McDowell on 'O Lucky Man!',
I think he suggested me for the role of his wife in 'Caligula'.
He wanted to have a friend around on this perilous film.
It was not an experience that I enjoyed particularly, but
it had its good points, one of which was the director,
Tinto Brass. He is a rambunctious, large-living man and I
loved him. His favourite place in the world at that time was
Soho, for there you could find all that was necessary in his
life: food, sex and films. He was also a founding member of
the Radical Party in Italy, whose political function was,
he said, 'To be the pepper in the arse of all the other
parties.' An excellent political aim. Buried in the mess that
is 'Caligula' is a bold, energetic film by Tinto. An enduring
memory of being on the set of 'Caligula' is my mother sitting
next to a huge gold phallus, chatting away to a three-
quarter-naked Italian male extra as if she was at the
bridge club. As I said, she could chat to anyone, anywhere.

A great portait of me in *Caligula*.

I was asked to act opposite the great Peter Sellers in what was to be his last film. The film was not good and disappeared without trace in the cinema, but gave me the opportunity to work with one of our geniuses of comedy. Peter and I got along very well. He was kind enough to laugh at my jokes, which was a great compliment coming from someone like him. This picture is from a visit I paid to him in hospital where he was recovering from a heart tremor. He could never resist a joke. Peter had a manservant/ assistant/costume designer/ friend called Michael Jeffries who was with him constantly. Michael knew everything there was to know about Peter, more than anyone including his wives and lawyers.

At the end of the shoot the ever-generous Peter gave me a lovely watch with the names of our two characters inscribed on the back: 'To Alice from Nayland'. Wearing it on my wrist while travelling back from Paris, this watch caused me to be arrested for smuggling and questioned for over five hours at the airport. I'd had no idea that the watch was solid gold. To escape jail time I had to pay virtually my entire salary in Customs duty. I shall never forget or forgive the bully who threatened, accused and questioned me at the airport. Later, at Stratford, this watch was stolen from my dressing room, just like the lovely gold chain given to me by James Mason.

Shortly after 'Caligula' I was asked to appear
in the film 'Excalibur', which has become a cult
film, loved by many. Again I had the fortune
to work with a brilliant costume designer, Bob
Ringwood, and met Liam Neeson, with whom
I lived for four happy years.

Above: Continuity Polaroids,
*A Midsummer Night's Dream*.
Previous pages: This is a contact sheet
of photos that I took of Liam for his
*Spotlight* photos. *Spotlight* is the
publication that casting directors use
in their search for actors for projects.
When Liam and I got together, and
he came to live with me in London,
he had only worked in Ireland. These
were some of the first steps that led
to his stardom.

My father died suddenly and while still grieving I was contracted to play Titania in 'Midsummer Night's Dream'. It was a role I had always wanted to play but which had eluded me, though I had played both Hermia and Helena, neither of which appealed to me. Because of my deep sadness over the loss of my father, I found it almost impossible to act. However I was helped by a great director, Elijah Moshinsky, a talented cast and a terrific wig, made at great expense out of hair that is extremely difficult to get hold of: pure, unbleached, very long, fine white-blonde hair. In wig-making terms, it was a work of art. Wigs are often such an important part of constructing a performance. As a performer I appreciate the brilliant craftspeople that construct both wigs and costumes, and owe them a great debt. Their work is done with the same commitment and passion as any actor. A performance can be either made or destroyed by these elements. In the case of my wig in the 'Dream', it made my performance, and I am grateful to it. Later this gorgeous piece was cut and dyed dark brown by the BBC wig department to be reused somewhere else. A terrible act of vandalism.

## The tribe of actors

One of the best parts of my working life has always been the actors and actresses I have spent time with. My profession allows people to be what they are. In my early days at Stratford there was sexism, and a lot of a kind of racism. Black or Asian actors were not given the chances they deserved. It is much better now, but still with some way to go. Not much has changed for the actresses. In general, however, the atmosphere in the theatre is one of freedom and acceptance, at least on a personal level. Also actors are the wittiest of people, inventive, imaginative and very intelligent. Male actors, in particular, are very funny, especially in a group. I have spent many days of my working life crying with laughter.

I get enraged by the lazy writing that brands actors shallow, silly, vain, or self-serving. The opposite is true. Actors have to be thoughtful as their job is to reflect the world around them. They have to be able to deconstruct complex language and ideas. They have to think not about the apparent meanings of plays, or scenes, or even a line, but what is buried beneath. They have to work collaboratively with many other people, technicians and craftspeople as well as writers, directors and other actors. They then have to face constant public criticism of their work.

We are also 'rogues and vagabonds' at heart. We are the tribe. It is what makes an actor what he or she is. It is nothing to do with being a 'star' or an egotist. Of course, that does exist in my profession, and a certain amount of egotism is essential to have the sheer courage to walk out on stage and perform. However, an out of control egotism, an exaggerated narcissistic self-absorption and vanity at the expense of others is very rare, in my experience.

Much more common, everyday in fact, is generosity, wit, intelligence, empathy, the love of company and encouragement. This is surprising because actors live in an intensely competitive world, where losing a job and someone else getting it means not being able to pay the rent. All actors face unemployment with regularity throughout their lives, so to behave generously to fellow actors is an act of altruism.

Often actors can find themselves working in conditions that no other worker, except maybe an illegal immigrant, would put up with. Very cramped, or unheated, dressing rooms or theatres, bathrooms five flights up, or rat-infested spaces, and they always keep their sense of humour and their resourcefulness.

I have worked with cast after cast of talented, amusing, inspiring people. Here are a small number of them and, at the risk of being called that horrible word, a 'luvvie', I am in fact exactly that, for I loved them all.

INKHEART

# America

*Hello Hollywood!*

**In 1982 Peter Hyams** was preparing to make *2010*, the sequel to Kubrick's masterpiece *2001*. The Thatcher years had taken hold in London and every restaurant in Parsons Green now seemed to be full of braying young male city types in pinstripe shirts, drunkenly throwing food at each other. The Greed Generation had arrived. It was fine to be venal, great to be greedy, fabulous to be voracious. Talk of global warming or green policies was met with utterly contemptuous condescension. I remember hearing a politician debating with Jonathon Porritt, who at that time was standing for the Green Party in my constituency. Porritt showed amazing forbearance in the face of the mocking and insulting tone taken by the other politician, a real product of the Thatcher approach. Finally Porritt said patiently, 'You may not be green now, but one day you will be because you will have to be. It is coming whether you like it or not.' Why did no one listen to him then? The information was out there, and maybe there was still time to make a difference.

That was one election where I really made an effort to get out and vote. I just did not like the direction my country and my city were going. I was not comfortable in the midst of all that. So when Peter Hyams asked me to play the Russian captain of a spacecraft, in a film to be shot in a studio in Los Angeles, I jumped at the chance. Please don't misunderstand: it wasn't that I thought the United States was 'greener' or less rapacious than Britain – far from it, as we all know. It was simply different, and not my country anyway.

The script was somewhat incomprehensible to me and the role not the best. The story was, however, prescient in that it foretold the joint American–Russian missions into space that happened after the collapse of Communism, although it did not foresee that collapse. In 1983, when the film was made, the Cold War was still in full swing. The script was also ahead of its time in giving a woman the job of captaining the spacecraft.

I arrived in Los Angeles and was given the keys to a brand-new Mustang convertible, and a second set of keys to a condo off the Sunset Strip. I was in heaven.

It soon became apparent that Peter had had no idea of my background when he cast me. When I met with him in LA, he wanted to hear my accent. Before leaving London I had done some preparation, taking dialogue lessons from a Russian girl who worked at the BBC World Service. I had it down pretty good, I thought. But Peter was unimpressed.

'I dunno, Helen. It just doesn't have the "nye" that I remember from my Russian grandparents.' I went home in despair and played back the tape of my work. It sounded good to me. Then the penny dropped. Peter, with his Russian Jewish roots, was used to an American Russian accent, whereas I was doing the accent of a Russian who had learned English in England. The next day I met with Peter again and this time put a hint of American into the accent. 'Yeah, that's it!' he said. 'That's a Russian accent!'

The rest of my spaceship crew were played by real Russians, so my accent came under heavy scrutiny. For the most part they were Russians who had got out because they were Jewish. Some had been well known in their homeland; one had been the most famous comedian in Russia. Now they were struggling small-part players in Hollywood. They were great to work with, intense, like all Russians. Their trailer would explode into shouts and thumping, and when I'd knock on the door to see what was happening, a massive, screaming argument would be in progress: Who was better, Gogol or Dostoevsky? The thumps were the table being thumped.

First thing in the morning, as the pink light of an LA dawn rose over the palm trees, I would drive, with the top of the Mustang down, to the studio lot. Down Crescent Heights till you can go no further, right to La Cienega, left on La Cienega to Washington, and Washington all the way to MGM studios. The famous logo of the roaring lion was still in place over the entrance.

MGM! Legendary home to Gable, Harlow, Garbo and Crawford. Judy Garland had walked those alleys with Fred Astaire and Gene Kelly. The studio we worked in held the covered-over tank that Esther Williams had gracefully dived into. In the dusty corners you could still see the boards that actresses wearing heavy costumes and headdresses would rest upon when unable to sit down. To me it was very imposing, very romantic. The security guard would say 'Good morning, Helen!'

I was given this cake when I won best actress at Cannes for *Cal*. Unfortunately, by the time I knew I had won it was too late to get there.

and I would drive to my allotted parking space. Then I would go to work on a stage that held the memories of all those ghosts. It possessed the same power as an empty theatre, a palpable feeling of creativity and the scent of successes and failures. I loved every minute.

Roy Scheider, my co-star, lived on the East Coast but loved the sun. He had a lounger set up outside his trailer and every day would take the rays as he waited for the set-up to happen. He got very brown over the months. This was the only film I have ever shot in sequence. It was possible to do it that way because the whole story takes place on the spacecraft, which was built on the stage. And if you look closely at the film you can see Roy slowly getting more and more tanned in space.

I had to learn that Americans did not go in for the kind of theatrical swearing I was used to. There is one word in particular which begins with a 'c' and ends with a 't' and has an 'n' and a 'u' in it. This word is absolutely the pits in America. No word is worse. Whereas in the theatrical culture I'd come from it's almost a term of endearment. I learned how appalling it is to utter this word on set one day. Roy was joking around and said something on my close-up to make me laugh. I did and the director called 'Cut!' As an amused throwaway, I turned to Roy and said, 'Oh, Roy, you c★★★.' The whole studio froze in horror. Roy looked utterly shocked, whereupon I dug myself in deeper and deeper. 'Oh no! Oh, I didn't mean you c★★★, I just meant, you know, you c★★★.' Roy forgave me, I hope. Later I tried to explain to him the disgusting nature of Luvvie Lingo in Britain.

My condo was situated on Hayvenhurst in a beautiful old apartment block. Bette Davis lived in the penthouse. One day I was swimming in the pool and looked up to see that unmistakable head peering down to see who was splashing about. The apartment was fiercely protected. You had to go through about five iron security doors to get into it. Tedious but safe. After a couple of days I realised that there was a rear exit leading directly from the terrace at the back of my apartment down some steps to a funky wooden door that opened directly on to the street. I was completely vulnerable. The stories of criminals with guns were scary, and every time I heard the police sirens go, which was quite often on the Strip, especially on a Saturday night, I would freeze in fear. After a month or so I relaxed and realised that I was not actually going to get shot. In fact, I was safer in Los Angeles than in my house in Parsons Green.

I also had good friends in LA. Brad Davis, whom I had met doing a piece for television, was a terrific mate. He and his wife had a house in the valley that became a meeting place for all kinds of people, from John Hurt to Ruby Wax. Brad was the most funny, charismatic, warm-hearted person, and I was honoured to call him my friend. I was sad when this gig came to an end, and the keys to the Mustang were taken away along with the keys to the condo. Determined to stay on in America, I rented an old banger from Rent-a-Wreck, a Mustang convertible again, only old and pink this time, and moved into the apartment of a girlfriend from England.

It was at this time that I learned I had been given the Best Actress award in Cannes for *Cal*. I'd known the film was playing there, for I had been invited to go, but the film company were not prepared to pay my way from LA and I didn't want to pay for myself. When news of the award came through they tried to get me there, but by then it was too late. Even with a private plane I could not have made it in time, so I missed a moment of glory. I won again in Cannes a few years later with *The Madness of King George* and again couldn't go, this time because I was working in the theatre. I was always rather sad about this, remembering that first trip to Cannes and wanting my moment of triumph on the Croisette.

Then I was called in to meet with a director who was preparing a film about Russia. His name was Taylor Hackford. I shrugged my shoulders. 'Oh well,' I thought, 'I guess they think I actually am Russian, from seeing *2010*.' The film was about two dancers, and starred Mikhail Baryshnikov and Gregory Hines. I was sent the script. The role was OK: head of the Kirov Ballet, someone who worked within the system. I took exception to certain elements in the script, which I thought reflected too closely American paranoia about Soviet Russia. I felt that not all Russians wanted to leave Russia and that there remained a deep love of country that was independent of the political system, but this was nowhere to be found in the script.

However I duly went off to meet with this director. I'd had a few meetings like this in LA and had found them always very intimidating and humiliating. There is a completely different attitude to a film audition in Los Angeles. It's a town where every waitress and barman wants to be a film star, so you as the actor are supposed to be incredibly grateful to be auditioning at all. You are one amongst a million. Next, the process has very little to do with acting. It's all to do with whether you are 'right' for the part. This is why actors and waiters and every other aspiring star dresses for the role when they go for an audition. If you show yourself to be 'right' for the part in your read-ing and you get cast, that's the end of the story. The performance you are required to give is what you did in the reading. They feel cheated if you then take it off in another direction.

This is the opposite of how I prefer to work. I want to change and experiment and invent. I want the freedom to use my imagination. There are as many ways of playing a line or a part as there are blades of grass. It is only poverty of imagination that stops you. So, actually, although I wanted to stay in America for the sense of personal freedom it gave me, I was not at all suited to the 'Hollywood' system.

So off I went to meet with Taylor Hackford, already slightly resentful and cross, and refusing to look anything like the head of the Kirov Ballet. Then he's late and I am waiting in the office, steaming now, glaring at the girl behind the desk. I am insulted. If I can get there on time, then he most certainly can. Fifteen minutes go by. I think, 'OK, I will wait for twenty minutes in total. That is the cut-off point.' A further five minutes go by and I stand up to leave, telling the alarmed secretary that I'm off. I walk to the door and, as I reach for the handle, Taylor walks in – and into the next twenty years of my life, and counting.

However that was not at all clear in this, our first meeting. Well, actually, our second. By now I am very pissed off and I show it. I hardly respond to anything, just wanting to get out of there.

Mikhail is there too, and, while I am very impressed to meet the greatest living dancer, I do not want to engage in small talk. 'So, do you want me to read?' I ask. I read the scene and when I'm done I say, 'OK? That's it.' And gather my stuff together to get out of there. It's then Taylor says to me, 'We've met before you know.'

'I don't think so,' I reply snottily.

'Yes' he says, 'in San Juan Bautista, while you were working with the Teatro Campesino. I came to watch. I am a friend of Danny Valdez.' I was amazed. There and then I knew I was not dealing with the normal kind of Hollywood film director. Most Hollywood film directors would not have sat in a dusty little town far from Beverly Hills watching an experimental theatre workshop. I left the meeting somewhat chastened. My assumptions had been all wrong. A few hours later Taylor called to tell me I had the role. I was not exactly over the moon, as I felt again that the role was flawed in the writing, but it was a job, and in another fully-fledged Hollywood movie.

The first preparation I did, thanks to Taylor's insistence that I do research, was to fly to Leningrad, as it was then called, for a few days. This turned out to be an extraordinary experience.

First I had to return to London. I got in touch with my friends at the World Service, to see if they had any contacts still in Moscow. I was told of a couple who had fled Russia in very dramatic circumstances a few years before. The young man, in preparation for their escape, had joined the merchant navy, in a position far below his level of education. He had spent two or three years working as a seaman. When finally he felt the moment was right, he smuggled his young wife on board. They had stockpiled sleeping tablets and she took some and hid in the tiny space below his bunk. Halfway through the journey, afraid she was dying, he had taken a terrible risk by carrying her, with difficulty, to the deck. There he hid her in a lifeboat. When the ship arrived in Hull, he dragged her ashore and begged asylum from an uncomprehending policeman. They were in real danger, for had they been spotted from the boat or forced back on board by the police, they would have faced a long spell in jail. Luckily the policeman managed to understand what they were saying and took them in.

I arranged to meet this couple, and discovered that the wife had a mother and father in Moscow that they were unable to communicate with. The parents had been punished for the actions of the child. This of course was how the Soviets controlled their citizens. If you tried to get away, it was your family who suffered. The reason Mikhail was able to leave was because he had no relatives in Russia, his mother having committed suicide.

The young couple had run away without thinking too much about the effect on their parents, but now they were desperate to be in touch. They gave me letters to smuggle in and safe numbers to call. The go-between was a friend of theirs who could be trusted and spoke some English. I was instructed to call only from a call box, not the hotel. They were deadly serious. The Soviet Union was in its darkest days of paranoia.

In those days, going into Russia your bags were searched more carefully than when you were leaving. The letters were burning a hole in the sock under my foot. I had also been given books in Russian for the parents; banned, as it turned out. I said they were for friends in Finland, where I was going after Russia. These were confiscated, but the letters got through, hidden in my shoe.

As soon as I could, I went to a call box and dialled the number. The young man who answered was very suspicious, but I persuaded him to meet me. He came, still suspicious, but gradually I was able to convince him that I was not a KGB agent and he set up a meeting with the parents.

The day came. I was instructed not to open my mouth in public, just to say 'Da' or 'Niet', and we took a taxi out to the sad Soviet-style outskirts of Leningrad, with huge ugly grey blocks made up of tiny apartments. The parents had been successful engineers with a nice apartment in the centre of Leningrad. Their punishment for their child escaping had been to lose their dacha, their jobs and their apartment.

Above: My pink
Mustang from Rent-a-
Wreck, the famous car-
rental company in LA.

Once they realised I was for real they were absolutely overjoyed to hear from their daughter and
son-in-law. I gave them the letters, plus an umbrella I had brought as a gift. I thought it was something
I could legitimately be seen to be carrying. There was much weeping and they were very kind to
me. I explained that I was in Leningrad to do research for my role and was hoping to visit the Kirov
(now the Maryinsky again), just to see what it was like. They said, 'We will arrange it.'

It turned out one of them had a brother who worked in the orchestra. I was told to meet them
around the corner from the theatre, and there they made the introduction. Again I was given strict
instructions not to open my mouth under any circumstances. The uncle then took me in through
the stage door, and showed me every inch of the backstage area, from the dressing rooms to the
beautiful rehearsal space on the top floor that Misha had described to Taylor. He did this despite
the risk to himself and his position. It was an act of great generosity and some courage. I was then
taken to a box seat where I watched the ballet. My research could not have been better.

In those memorable days in Leningrad, with these new friends, it was so clear that the days of
the Soviet regime were numbered. It was writ large. The young people I met were absolutely fed
up with the system. They did not care about the Second World War and the struggles against the
Nazis, the siege of Leningrad or the twenty-two million dead. They did not care about equality
or owning the means of production. They wanted blue jeans and rock and roll. They wanted to
hear the music they wanted to hear and wear the clothes they wanted to wear, and read the books
they wanted to read. They wanted cultural freedom. Soviet Communism was doomed. The next
year Gorbachev came into power and perestroika began.

In 2004 I returned to Russia. Leningrad had reverted to St Petersburg, and this time when I
met with the parents it was in the open, in a restaurant where we could speak freely. It was a wonderful reunion. Their daughter and son-in-law had been back several times, and the parents had
visited London. Life was better for them, and it was wonderful to see.

From Russia I flew to Finland and started work on *White Nights*, and also started on a relationship that is still with me.

Two of my greatest friends in Los Angeles were Brad Davis
and his wife. Brad had a sauna in the garden shed of his
house in Studio City, and he would force all visitors in
there. Brad was a great free spirit, and anyone who knew
him treasured him. When I first met him, on a film for
television, he had come out of rehabilitation from going
AWOL with drink and drugs. He'd had a great success
with 'Midnight Express' and could not handle that and
the pressures of Hollywood. Once he was over that glitch,
which almost destroyed his career (Brad never did
anything by halves), he was a wicked angel of a person.

I had to come from Fulham for this Command
Performance, attended by Charles and Diana. With my
friend Sandy I left with plenty of time, as we had strict
instructions to arrive for the screening before the Royal
party. However I did not reckon with Fulham football
ground. They were playing at home that Saturday, and just
as we left for the theatre the fans came out. My car got
stuck in horrendous traffic. The only way to get to the
Leicester Square Theatre on time was to bail out of the car
and run the last 500 yards. Sandy and I ran, jumped the
security fence, and arrived panting and sweating seconds
before Charles and Diana.

Film stills from *2010*.

Here are the two
faces of love. One
acted and one real.
Work it out.

In the background of the shot of me and Tay talking is
camera operator Freddie Cooper. Taylor said he was
astounding to work with, the best he had ever known. His
eye was brilliant, his technique superlative. Filming dance is
notoriously difficult, but Freddie's camera seemed to be
able to anticipate to within an eighth of an inch where
Misha or Gregory Hines's foot would land, and arrive at
that spot in a smooth, imperceptible move.

# In Front of the Camera

*Moving up a level and Jane Tennison*

**I feel as though it took me** for ever to learn how to act for the screen. Even now, I am still not sure that I have cracked it. When I was starting out, I could not look at myself, it made me feel too self-conscious. The way your mouth moves, the sound of your voice, the set of your head from behind, and a million other things completely take you by surprise. It is a very uncomfortable feeling. Also the knowledge that this piece of shadow and light will come back to haunt you for years to come is very intimidating. My acting then was so 'rabbit in the headlights' I preferred not to look at it unless absolutely necessary.

When I did *Mosquito Coast* I was determined to use the experience as a tool to free me. Film acting, at its best, combines a sense of utter freedom within a discipline that is highly technical and controlled. I have watched it at its best. My husband made a film with Al Pacino and I was impressed by how technically adept Al was, knowing precisely the camera angles, the lenses, the continuity, the correct pitch for the close-up, the medium shot, the wide, and so forth, and yet he managed to remain absolutely free and improvisational within those confines.

When I did *Mosquito Coast* I had not yet had the advantage of watching Al at work. I had, however, done *2010*, and worked with an actor called Bob Balaban, and he gave me some invaluable advice that I have used ever since. He said film acting is like archery. You aim the arrow and hope it will hit its target, but you can never be sure of that. You have to just let it go, and leave it to fall where it will. 'Never go home and angst about what you might have or should have done,' he said. 'You cannot take it back, so just let it go.'

Finding myself in the jungles of Belize, with another consummate technician, Harrison Ford, I decided to ignore the technical side for the time being and just learn to be as free as possible, just be, or try to be.

I have always said my inspirations for film acting are babies and animals, for they behave with no awareness of the camera at all. Well, actually animals, babies and Anna Magnani. Behaviour is really what film acting is about, which is why sometimes you will find great film actors who cannot perform on stage. I drove Peter Weir, the director, mad with my lack of technique, 'behaving' away with no consciousness of where the camera was, let alone what lens was being used, often not on camera at all. I didn't care. I just wanted to be free. In fact, this experience was very useful for me, and it broke the fear I had of those black machines about to capture your soul.

So this was the beginning of my education in film acting. It continued through every film I subsequently did, but it was not until the relentless hours of work that I put into *Prime Suspect* that I became a graduate. I had the advantage of working very closely with some superb directors who understood their medium and its techniques. They all taught me as I watched them work. Whenever possible I would spend time behind the camera, hovering with my ears open and, mostly, my mouth shut, eavesdropping as the director and cameraman or DP (director of photography) would have their discussions about how to shoot the scene. Afterwards I would go home and, as a relief from learning my lines, draw diagrams of how to shoot a scene with multiple characters, and what crossing the line is. I learned to ask the camera crew what lens was being used, I learned how important the dolly grip is, and how to work directly with all of the crew to make their jobs and my own easier.

The cast of the first *Prime Suspect*.

I think in all I did twenty-six onscreen hours of *Prime Suspect* and I came out the other end with a very good knowledge of all the morgues around Manchester and some in London, and a good understanding of film acting and film-making. I had learned to trust my instinct. I had learned freedom … I hope. It is still elusive.

*Prime Suspect* came my way like any other, with my agent sending me a script. I wish I could say I knew immediately that this was going to be an important part of my professional life, but I didn't. I did know that it was a terrific role: a funny, flawed real woman at last, one that was the protagonist in the story, the motor that drove it along. This was and still is very rare. Lynda La Plante, coming from her success with *Widows*, was writing with confidence and invention. The woman she wrote was perhaps the first I had ever read – and in that I include Shakespeare and Chekhov – that was not a fantasy figure of some sort, but seemed to be a woman I could recognise.

I met with Lynda and the executive producer, Sally Head. I think we were lucky in that the head of drama at that time was a woman, and the very talented Sally Head to boot, responsible for developing both *Prime Suspect* and, later, *Cracker*.

I happily agreed to have my hair cut, did a costume fitting, and met with a policewoman to learn a little about a world I knew nothing about, the world of the police.

Fresh from the costume fitting, where I had been posing in front of the mirror assuming what I thought was a strong position – arms folded, butch-looking … you know – I met with the woman in charge of Holloway police station. She gave me the most invaluable advice: never let them see you cry, and never cross your arms. When I asked why, she said, 'Because it is a defensive action and therefore weak.' The police are masters when it comes to body language. She went on to tell me that, if you want to show power over someone, you should touch him or her lightly on the arm. Watch heads of state as they meet each other; they fight to be the first one to touch. Throughout *Prime Suspect* I don't think I ever crossed my arms, and Jane Tennison only cries in private.

I then had to fly off to Italy to film *Where Angels Fear to Tread*. It was one of those occasions where the scheduling of two projects is so tight they almost overlap. At 4 p.m. when the film finished shooting in Tuscany, I drove for three hours to the nearest airport, got home at about 11 p.m. and was due on set to start shooting the next day in London at 6 a.m., the first order of business being to have my hair cut. I had absolutely no preparation time, diving in at the deep end. I simply had to play it by ear, so to speak, and rely on my instincts.

My real worry was how I was going to learn it. It seemed a vast amount to get in my head. I had never played in a four-hour piece with such a long role before. In the early thoughts about a part, you have to have a sense of the overall shape of the performance. What happens in the beginning and how you play it has to make sense and have a connection to what happens in the end. The character shifts and learns and changes through the story, and that should be seen.

In film-making this process is messed up by shooting completely out of sequence. You often start shooting the very last scene, then jump to the middle, then to the beginning, then back to the end again. Therefore it is essential to have a very clear sense of how the character is developing through the story.

Just to organise the script was intimidating, especially with no preparation time. On my days off in Italy I would psychologically drag myself out of turn-of-the-century Italian society into a dark contemporary world and struggle with the huge, unwieldy script. To begin with I tried breaking the script down into scenes and sticking them up around my hotel room, but I quickly ran out of wall space.

In the end, once work on *Prime Suspect* was under way, I found a system of learning that divided upcoming scenes into folders marked 'tomorrow', 'day after tomorrow' and 'next week', broken down into days of the week. It is a system I have used ever since, learning scenes two to three days ahead. Whenever I was not actually filming, I was learning. I was so happy to throw pages away as they had been filmed.

Chris Menaul, the director, had a very strong visual style he wanted to achieve. Without being too technical, this involved a camera that was always moving, slowly with long lenses.

A *very* small selection of photographs from *Prime Suspect* over the years!

It gave the piece a very atmospheric look, but was devilishly difficult to achieve for all concerned, actors and camera crew.

I think we went through three focus pullers on that first show. The depth of field was very shallow, almost impossible for the focus puller, and required very accurate hitting of marks by the actors. One inch over the mark and you would be out of focus. A further problem was the fact that we were filming in winter in Maxwell House, former home of the Maxwell publishing empire in Manchester. Unheated, freezing cold and rat-infested – that human rat having been replaced by more innocent four-legged rodents – it was not a building that was designed to be filmed in. The moving camera would squeak its way over the wooden floors, destroying the soundtrack of any take that was in focus. We all had to be very, very patient. We also came under pressure from the production company, Granada, for budgetary reasons. I don't think there was much belief in the project, there being a suspicion that a female-led drama could not succeed.

Chris Menaul earned my admiration for the dogged and relentless way he pressed on, refusing to compromise his vision, no matter how hard it was to achieve. That is all you want from a film

Right: With Harrison Ford in *Mosquito Coast*.
Centre: This display from a video store in Georgia was the closest I ever got to equal billing with a big movie star.
Bottom: Some of my co-stars and our driver. I especially loved the two red-headed twins playing my daughters.

director, an obsessed and uncompromisingly relentless nature, combined with a great technical ability. In Chris, we had exactly those qualities, and the ultimate success of *Prime Suspect* came from his vision and his insistence in getting it on the screen.

Surprisingly, considering the subject matter and the circumstances of the shoot, I found myself in a situation of almost constant laughter, thanks to the fantastic cast that Doreen Jones, the casting director, had assembled with Chris. The men and woman who played the team of detectives were not for the most part seasoned television actors, but Doreen had a knack of finding very talented, interesting actors, and in the process discovered quite a few stars.

Tom Bell, who made such an impression on the audience with his wonderful performance as the bitter, mean and sexist Bill Otley, was of course a well-known actor, but also in that cast list you will find the names of Tom Wilkinson, Zoë Wanamaker and Ralph Fiennes. To me every actor working on that first *Prime Suspect* was a star.

It was my team – the fellow actors playing detectives that I spent so many hours with and who made it all so much easier for me with their support and their sense of fun – that I shall never forget and always be grateful for. The cast of *Prime Suspect 1* are special people.

When I signed up for the series my contract stated that Granada would do one, put it out to see how it would play, and then, if successful, I was to do two more. At this point no one, least of all me, had any idea whether this drama would succeed, not understanding that in a way it could not fail, for it was truly ground-breaking.

I think one of the reasons for the success of *Prime Suspect* was Lynda's understanding of how things had changed. We were sick of the characters we saw on the screen depicting our world. There was no recognition of where women were. Women had come out of college education in the sixties, the first generation to have that opportunity regardless of their economic background, and entered the workplace as doctors, lawyers, teachers, businesswomen, engineers or policewomen, and had encountered a great deal of resistance to their presence from male colleagues. They had had to eat shit, and keep quiet about it, for to complain just pushed you further back down the ladder.

There was now a silent but angry mass of these women out there. Successful professional women who wanted the world to see what they had had to put up with. *Prime Suspect* fitted the bill perfectly. Lynda had also come up with a hard-hitting, brutal story with testosterone appeal, so the men had to watch it as well. It had the double whammy of relevant social comment and a thrilling storyline. It was a combination that was maintained throughout the subsequent series of *Prime Suspect*, or at least aimed towards.

The first indication I got that it might be a winner came from my nephew, Simon. Now a successful writer and producer of television drama in the States, he was then making a living as a plasterer and writing in his spare time.

I sent him off to see the screening and check it out for me. I've always found it hard to watch myself. It is hard to be objective, and as much as I want to see the director's work, I am so hyper-critical of myself that it gets in the way. Simon was a true South London boy, and I knew he would tell me the truth.

He loved it. 'It's great, Hel. I mean it. You don't have anything to worry about.'

After that I went off to meet the press. They kind of liked it, but I did not get the impression of a huge hit. Maybe they were shell-shocked.

Even with Simon's approbation, I never expected the kind of response we eventually got. It became, in TV parlance, 'water-cooler television', the must-see programme people talked about at work. It also got sensational reviews. Granada began talks about when I might be available to do the next one.

Production stills from Peter Greenaway's *The Cook, the Thief…*(1989). Left, playing the 'solemnly sexy' Georgina.

I was playing Arthur Miller's 'Two-Way Mirror' at the Young Vic when I started filming. I would get to the studio, film all day, be off at 5 p.m, and drive to the theatre for 6 p.m to get ready for the evening performance. I was absolutely exhausted, but it was also one of the most fun shoots to work on, thanks to the high spirits of the cast. Again, we laughed all day. I instituted something I called 'breakfast', which was one bottle of champagne every morning at make-up, shared by all ten or so of us. Just a quarter of a glass, enough to make you feel faintly giggly on an empty stomach. We would dance on to the set in the highest of spirits. The entire budget had gone on making the food for the set look great. It was cooked and presented by the top sous-chef at the Dorchester. We actors, of course, were not allowed to touch it. By comparison our food was awful: spam and cheap cheese. The dog turds used in that horrific first scene were also made by our chef. He prepared them out of the very best chocolate, like beautiful chocolate truffles. The minute the dogs were let out, they ran around and ate them all up. Once again, the actors missed out!

Above: With Nigel
Hawthorne in *The Madness
of King George* (1994).
Opposite top: With
Amanda Donohoe on set.
Opposite bottom: A
continuity Polaroid.

My first queen on screen. It fitted perfectly
with my love of costume. I also got to work with
Nigel Hawthorne, one of the real gentlemen of stage
or screen. I admired his constant patience and
energy, and later when I played Elizabeth I and
I was flagging or tired, I would remember Nigel's
unfailing commitment, and pull myself together. He
was nominated for an Oscar for his performance.
On the day of the Oscars, he was very happy. He
had worked towards this for so many years with a

long history of really consummate work. Then the 'Mail and the 'Express' in Britain decided to 'out' him in a mean-spirited and bitchy way. Nigel was devastated, his great day utterly destroyed. The cruellest part of this was that Nigel had always been totally candid about his sexuality, and had lived openly and happily with his partner, Trevor Bentham, for many years. This story in fact came from an open interview Nigel had given to the 'Advocate', a gay magazine. It was a spiteful, malicious attack on a gracious, hard-working and very talented actor, all for the sake of a cheap headline. Shame on them.

Working with Robert Altman was unlike any other filming experience. His approach to the medium was a perfect blend of freedom and improvisation with control and organisation. I think he loved working in Britain, with a cast of star actors who nonetheless came from our traditions of ensemble and discipline. We all adored him and loved working on the film. A mark of his brilliance was that he was halfway through shooting the film when he suddenly decided to make Eileen Atkins and myself sisters. He shot the whole upstairs sequences first and then the downstairs, and therefore, as I almost only ever appeared downstairs, I was not required until halfway through the shoot. At the halfway point, I came in and got into costume for the cast and crew photo. I sat down and joined Eileen and Bob for lunch. Bob suddenly looked at the two of us and said, 'I have an idea, why don't we make the two of you sisters, what do you think?' We couldn't see any reason not to, so he called the writer, Julian Fellowes, over and suggested it. Julian agreed and an important part of the plot was invented there and then. He always had a point of view of a scene that was not obvious, playing it on a non-speaking role like a dog's progress through legs, or the sleepy faces of the young servants. He also had a way of shooting with two cameras that were constantly on the move, so you never knew if you were on camera or not. It kept you on your toes.

*Gosford Park* (2001).
Opposite: 'Upstairs'.
Far left: Clive Owen
as Robert Parks.
Left: As Mrs Wilson
(housekeeper, and
revealed to be
Robert Parks's
mother).
Below: The
'downstairs cast'.

Above: *Teaching Mrs Tingle* (1999).
Left: *Losing Chase* (1996).
Below: With Jack Nicholson as the veteran police detective in *The Pledge* (2001).
Opposite: With Robert Redford in *The Clearing* (2004).

With the success of 'Prime Suspect' in America,
I slowly became someone to cast in movies.
Luckily some of my fans were film-makers like
Kevin McDonald, Kevin Bacon who directed
'Losing Chase' and Robert Redford.

Three of the best roles I have played on film
have never been seen in the UK. 'The Passion of
Ayn Rand', Mrs Stone in 'The Roman Spring
of Mrs Stone' and 'Door to Door'. They played
on American cable TV and won acclaim there.

Opposite: In Vivien
Leigh's role as Karen
Stone in *The Roman
Spring of Mrs Stone*
(2003), with Olivier
Martinez.
Right: In *The Passion
of Ayn Rand*.
Below: With the
cast and director of
*The Roman Spring
of Mrs Stone*.

It was on the read-through of this film that I realised what a wonderful experience it was going to be. To hear those actresses doing their thing, all of them on top of their game, with a brilliance combined with modesty that only women and Brits, at that, can muster. It only got better from there. As a woman on a film set or in the theatre you are always outnumbered by men. It was so refreshing to be one of a large cast of women. We had a grand time, behaving like girls do. I loved every minute. My only difficulty, and this was a very hard one, was that just before I started the film I received a call from my brother in the Philippines. He had been diagnosed with melanoma cancer, from his days in the African sun. He also had no medical insurance and refused to leave Manila, which was now his home. In Manila there is no health service and no understanding in the medical world for this cancer. The Philippines just don't get it. It is a white person's cancer. Early every morning, with the time zone difference, I would be speaking with doctors and trying to arrange operations and care for my brother. I spoke to him almost every day and could hear his decline. I would then go on to the set and play a light comedy. I could not share my burden with any of my fellow actresses as I did not want to cast a sad spell over their work. The only person I told was Nigel Cole, our sensible and sensitive director. On the day my brother died we were shooting a funeral scene and my tears were put to use. 'Calendar Girls' was one of the best of my film experiences, thanks to the rest of the cast, and at the same time one of the darkest.

Squeezing a bountiful harvest

# JANUARY · 2004

| SUNDAY | MONDAY | TUESDAY | WEDNESDAY | THURSDAY | FRIDAY | SATURDAY |
|---|---|---|---|---|---|---|
| | | | | NEW YEAR'S DAY | NEW YEAR'S HOLIDAY (CANADA, NZ) | |
| 28 | 29 | 30 | 31 | 1 | 2 | 3 |
| 4 | 5 | 6 | 7 | 8 | 9 | 10 |
| 11 | 12 | 13 | 14 | 15 | 16 | 17 |
| | MARTIN LUTHER KING JR. DAY (US) | | | | | |
| 18 | 19 | 20 | 21 | 22 | 23 | 24 |
| | AUSTRALIA DAY (AUS) | | | | | |
| 25 | 26 | 27 | 28 | 29 | 30 | 31 |
| 1 | 2 | 3 | 4 | 5 | 6 | 7 |

# My Amazing Year

*Playing queens, saying goodbye to Jane Tennison and winning an Oscar*

**My amazing year** was actually more like eighteen months. It was the year I actually did the work that would lead to many red carpets and endless interviews.

It began with a film called *Shadowboxer* that was shot in Philadelphia. A couple of years earlier I had been walking along Houston Street in downtown New York, minding my own business, trying to avoid the many potholes in the pavement, when I was accosted by an outrageous and effervescent person, black and rather beautiful with a fantastic head of wild dreads. He said, 'You don't know me, but I am a film producer and I think you are great. I would love to work with you some time.' I was polite and went on my way, loving the fact that someone as cool looking as that would think I was good, but also not imagining for a second that he was for real. Well, he was. His name, as I found out two years later, was Lee Daniels, and he was the producer responsible for a very good film called *Monster's Ball* that had taken Halle Berry to an Oscar the year my husband was nominated for *Ray*. I had seen her weep her way through her speech and wept with her. Her reaction was irresistible.

Lee sent me a script called *Shadowboxer*, by the writer of *Monster's Ball*, that he wished to direct as a first-time director. The role was fantastic: a professional assassin, dying of cancer, locked in a relationship with her stepson with whom she worked. My stepson was to be played by Cuba Gooding Jnr, an extra dimension that was likely to upset certain people. I was to wear only Vivienne Westwood. Of course I agreed. I made the film, and had a grand time with Cuba, of course, but also Macy Gray, Mo'Nique, Stephen Dorff, and I got to meet Jay-Z, Lenny Kravitz and various hip-hop and rap artists who visited the set. Lee made an original and stylish film that came and went pretty fast in the cinema. I think really only the black community saw it in America. Certainly many black people come up to me in the States, recognising me from that film, not anything else. It then went to video. However, as far as I was concerned it was the first achievement of my amazing year.

About a year and a half before this I had met with the brave and independent producers of Company Pictures, George Faber and Charlie Pattinson, and with the writer Nigel Williams. They had asked if I was interested in doing a four-hour piece about Elizabeth I, concentrating on the second half of her life and her inappropriate relationship with Essex. What actress would ever say no to that?

Nigel went away and wrote a draft. The producers and I then gave our thoughts on it. He went away and come up with another brilliant draft and we all agreed we could go ahead. I suggested the director, Tom Hooper, who had directed my previous *Prime Suspect*, amongst many other prestigious dramas, and both the producers and the writer agreed. All that was needed was the financing. Channel 4 declared an interest and then we had the great good luck of HBO, the American cable channel, coming on board. I think we had the advantage of the head of HBO being a Brit, Colin Callendar. Tom assembled an astounding cast, lead by Jeremy Irons, Hugh Dancy, Toby Jones, Patrick Malahide and Ian McDiarmid.

For a project of this type, the budget was tiny, so it was decided to shoot the piece in Lithuania. This is the kind of practical decision that producers have to make. There we are, making a film about the most iconic queen in British history, and we have to shoot it in Lithuania. But the sets could be built more cheaply there, and the remnants of a post-Soviet film industry would supply labour. So away we went. Summer in Lithuania is very hot and humid. It is a beautiful country with lakes and forests, virtually untouched by Soviet development, which has saved it ecologically. However, I did not get to see much of that because my filming schedule left no room for sightseeing.

Getting ready for my close-up!

One of the problems of working in Lithuania was that we needed a lot of extras. We found them easily enough, but they spoke no English and had no idea who Elizabeth I was. They were sweet and hard-working, but understandably not very committed to our history. There were communication problems too. A quarter of the way through the shoot I discovered that the Bulgarian second assistant was ordering them around in Russian, which wasn't helping matters. Given the history between Lithuania and Russia, they loathed the Russian language and deeply resented being told what to do in it. I tried to smooth troubled waters. When we came to shoot the famous 'body of a woman but heart of a king' speech, the responding cheers were very half-hearted. The extras playing the troops massed at Dover to fight off the looming Spanish invasion were tired and wet after standing in the rain all day. Knowing that the Lithuanians adore basketball, I explained that they should react as if their team had won the world cup. They leapt into life and gave me a rousing cheer. A Lithuanian lip reader would be able to see the name of the team on their lips.

My costumes were very hot and heavy, and my trailer was too far away to rest there between takes. I was on set all day every day, my back aching from the weight of the elaborate gowns I had to wear. Tom, the producers and I decided to work through the day with no lunch break, as this at least meant we could break at a reasonable hour and have some kind of evening. It also meant that the crew worked eleven-hour days with no break, other than what they could snatch. I don't think anyone outside the business can quite comprehend the kind of work put in by a film crew under these circumstances. I appreciated the Herculean efforts being achieved by the crew and tried to stand toe to toe with them. I then had to go home and learn lines at the end of the day. It was relentless.

However, I knew that this was the best role I would ever play, and I was determined to give it everything I could. I had read a piece about Vivien Leigh realising that *Gone with the Wind* was the best thing she would ever do, and being alive with the energy to perform it. I felt like that. No tiredness, pain or fear was going to stop me giving it all the technique, passion and instinct I had. We had to shoot fast, so there was not much time to do more than one or two takes.

It was almost all shot on a steady-cam, which was an efficient and visceral way to shoot, but also technically demanding. The steady-cam operator, Peter Cavaciuti, was incredible. His strength alone, carrying that heavy piece of equipment all day in the heat and then making extraordinary shots, was heroic. Also Tom Hooper showed the qualities that had made me want to work with him again: an indefatigable and unremitting commitment to his work. We became a team in trying to get the material in the camera in focus and in a well-shaped shot, yet full of life, energy and detail. I also found it moving that, there I was, maybe four hundred miles west of the Kuryanovo estate where my grandfather had been born and spent his youth.

When you do work in film, television or theatre you have no idea of the ultimate result. You don't know if the work will be loved or loathed. The heartbreaking side to television drama is that you all work so hard, give it so much, with high levels of expertise in many different disciplines – writing, production, design, acting, directing, costume design, music composition, camera work, lighting, props, set dressing, etc., etc. – and then when it goes out the critics mention it in the same breath as the latest episode of *Wife Swap*. It can be very disheartening. However, *Elizabeth* got just about the best reviews I have ever received in Britain, and went on to be similarly lauded in America, winning almost every award available to it there. In Britain it was inexplicably totally shut out from the BAFTAs.

The next job was *The Queen*. A couple of years earlier, Andy Harries had seduced me back to *Prime Suspect* by making me realise that I was in the best of hands with him on board as executive producer. When I saw the writers and directors that he had gathered, I knew the quality of work he was aiming towards. Both the writer, Peter Barry, and Tom Hooper, the director, were the creators the subject matter needed. When the time had come for the first cast meeting, where we would read through the script from beginning to end (the only time all the participants get to hear the whole script), I had arrived early in order to greet the cast as they arrived. I knew from personal experience how intimidating this kind of read-through can be and I wanted everyone to be at ease. Andy, who had also got there early, was at the other end of the room, watching. It occurred to him that I was being approached as if I were the Queen. Unfortunately, not the effect I was hoping for. He then thought I actually looked rather like the Queen. Then the light bulb went on in his head: How about doing a film with Helen playing the Queen.

When he presented the idea to me, my heart dropped, let alone my jaw. I thought it was the maddest notion, plus I was terrified. To play a living person is very intimidating; you can never be as good as the real person and if you are bad, then you are just bad. Also, this was the Queen, with all the colossal interest and confused, contradictory emotions that the monarchy arouses in our nation's hearts and minds. I thought I was headed for the most almighty embarrassing fall. So again I had to do it.

Andy quickly put the whole thing into action, bringing writer Peter Morgan and director Stephen Frears into the project. The process of getting the script and setting the film up took another year or so, but finally we were set to go. The final draft was a work of art. Spare, intelligent and unexpectedly poetic. It was the scene with the stag that took me by surprise and lifted the story into something more than pure documentary. It also made me sure that I wanted to do this film. Andy had brought Miramax, the distribution company, into partnership, a great move for the ultimate success of the film. Again we were helped by fact that the head of Miramax, Daniel Battsek, was an expatriate Brit.

When the roles of Elizabeth I and II were first proposed there was no certainty of them being made at all, let alone in the same year, let alone one straight after the other. However, that was the way the cards fell, and I was stunned when I realised this was how it was to be. My research had to be crammed into a two-week break between finishing *Elizabeth I* and the start of filming on *The Queen*. I have a funky old farmhouse in the South of France, and I locked myself away there with a suitcase full of tapes about the Queen, and sat for hours in front of the tiny ten-inch TV, studying her. I had already done some work with the dialect coach, Penny Dyer, before going to Lithuania. She is a genius, coming at the voice and accent through psychology. My work with her was invaluable. Though I never actually got the Queen's voice quite right, that was my inadequacy, not Penny's. In a way, it didn't matter.

Watching those tapes, I found myself drawn more and more to Elizabeth as a girl. I kept coming back to who she was before she had any understanding of the role she was to endure. Of course she was protected and living in a rarefied world; the wealthy daughter of an aristocrat back when those things mattered deeply in Britain. She inhabited the summit of a society that crushed people like my parents, or rather kept them firmly in place. It wasn't a world I was enamoured with. In the Silver Jubilee year I had had a Sex Pistols attitude to the Royal Family. However, there was such sweetness there in that person, such concern for others, such a sense of being a 'good' girl, exercising self-discipline and doing what you had to do, that I basically fell in love with the human. She also had the best of smiles.

I was still very nervous, unsure of whether I could do it, when I suddenly felt liberated by the idea that all I was doing was a portrait of her, the way a painter might. I had studied portraits of Elizabeth I because that was all I had for a physical reference. So I also looked at paintings of the present queen, to see what different artists may have seen in her. I thought that I did not have to do the most perfect impersonation, just my personal impression, fed by my own perceptions, as a painter does.

The building blocks of the performance were my work with Penny, my work in France, and then the costume fittings with Consolata Boyle, the costume designer. When I first saw the costumes laid out, my heart dropped. I am a girly woman, who loves dressing up. That has always been one of my greatest pleasures in my profession. On that level, Queen Elizabeth I was my ideal role, with endless big dresses and loads of jewellery. Here were tweed skirts and sensible brown shoes, Hermès and Barbour. I honestly did not think I could get my head around someone who chose of her own free will to wear that stuff, as expensive and beautifully made as it is. I reckoned without the inexplicable enchantment of the personality of Elizabeth. Wearing her clothes, I realised that this is a woman, unlike me, without vanity, and with a sense of practicality in her clothing. I wore a tiny bit of padding, put on those clothes and walked out into our communal garden to show the neighbours. Out of nowhere, or maybe out of the hours of watching tape, or simply out of the effect the clothes had on me, I slipped into her walk and into her head and found it to be the most comfortable place to be. From then on I loved wearing those clothes and shoes, loved being that character that I thought of as the captain of a submarine, deep and in control, but with a kind of simplicity.

We shot the film mostly in Scotland, where I know the producers had difficulty finding a big estate willing to allow us to shoot. There was a closing of ranks amongst the landowners against these presumptuous film-makers. I think the estate we ultimately shot in was owned by Americans who had no such compunction. The scene with the live stag was shot with the most terrible stuffed thing as my eyeline. It kept being put up and then laid down again with its legs in the air. It was difficult not to giggle. The later scene with the dead stag was shot with a real decapitated animal. It was much easier to be emotional.

The tone of the film was difficult to pin down, and none of us knew how to end it. Fortunately, we had Stephen's sense of humour and intelligence both working for us. The final scene had to be both funny and moving, and at the same time believable. I think it was a case of trial and error, with no absolute plan. We did have that great script, however, and a brilliant director. Even so, when the film was finished and edited it became clear to the producers that something was missing. Nothing is easy. Some new scenes were written by Peter, featuring Tony Blair, played with inspiration by Michael Sheen. It was better, but still needed something. That something was a tiny peep into the heart of Elizabeth, a woman who above all hides her feelings. Peter found this scene difficult to write. I sent in my suggestions and together we wrote a scene that was shot six months after the principal photography had wrapped. It was then spliced into the end of the film. The wonderful score by Alexandre Desplat was added, and finally *The Queen* was finished. As with all films, as we shot it there was no understanding of the impact the film might eventually have.

After that primary filming schedule I was almost immediately on to *Prime Suspect: the Final Act*. By then I was very tired, so it was just as well that Jane Tennison had demons to struggle with and could look awful. Again Andy had brought together a new and inspiring team in Philip Martin, the director, and Frank Deasy, the writer. He had previously asked if I would go one more round with this series, and I thought yes, but that this would be the last time.

I had imagined that I would be very sad to be playing this iconic role for the last time, but in reality I felt strongly that it was the right time to end. Whenever I had played Jane in the past, I had slipped into her like putting on an old and comfortable coat, worn around the edges and utterly familiar. This time was no different. I was pleased that, thanks to Andy, we could finish the story of Jane Tennison in a realistic and complete way. All along the series had fought towards realism and relevance, and the last episode was no different. The last day was shot as my last day on the force. By then, after eleven weeks of a hard schedule, I think we were all too tired to think of the implications, but Philip with his great sense of humour made it a good day and an easy one to get through.

So *Prime Suspect* ended, and with it my brilliant year. Then began the crazy year when all these projects were launched on the public.

Film stills from
*Shadowboxer.*

I began my brilliant year as a criminal and ended it
as the person who would have tracked me down, the
redoubtable Jane Tennison. It was hard to step away
from this role that had been in my life since 1991.
However, I felt it was time. I was also very tired by
then, having done 'Elizabeth I' and 'The Queen' back
to back. You can see it on my face here. Luckily I
did not have to look good, as Jane was struggling with
alcohol by now.

Left: In costume.
Below left: Pete,
our miraculous
cameraman.
Below: A make-
up test.
Opposite:
Learning lines.
Overleaf:
*Elizabeth I.*

This is how I looked any time I was not actually
filming on 'Elizabeth I'. I did not have time to get
back to my trailer, so would find a quiet corner and
try to get Nigel Williams' great words into my brain. The
most difficult lines to learn were Elizabeth's own words
which Nigel had masterfully incorporated into the text.
He was rightfully nominated for an Emmy for his work.

I don't think I have ever felt so comfortable playing a character as I did with Elizabeth II. This is strange, because we have nothing much in common, either in background or in interests. I think the comfort came from a love for and respect for all the people of her generation, no matter what their status. It is my parents' generation. In the sixties I wanted to get away from that generation as much as anyone else. I wanted to overturn and throw out what I saw as the restrictions and narrow-mindedness of the fifties. Now I see that generation in particular as heroes who gave up their youth for a better world. Also I must confess I loved the corgis.

The two sides of the
red carpet...

When 'The Queen' premiered at the Venice Film
Festival it was the first time it had been shown
to an audience. The film-makers are seated right
at the top of a flight of stairs that bisects the
auditorium. It is a very exposed position if the
film does not go down well - impossible to beat
a hasty and anonymous retreat. Likewise, if the
film goes well, you must sit or stand and accept
the applause, not such a hardship. If an Italian
audience likes a film, they give it a standing
ovation. At the end of 'The Queen' the audience
stood and applauded for what seemed like a
long time. Then, overwhelmed by the moment, I
raised my arms like an opera star. Actually, as
I did it, I thought to myself 'What the hell
are you doing, Helen - playing Evita?' As soon
as I could, I put my arms down again, very
embarrassed. My husband now can easily bring
me down a peg or two by quietly humming
'Don't cry for me, Argentina' . . .

Here is another side of
the work of an actress –
and it is work.

You win some and you lose some. That's how Robert Allan Ackerman, director of 'The Roman Spring of Mrs Stone', and I felt on losing the Emmy to 'Angels in America'. Felicity Huffman, so proud that 'Door to Door', produced by and starring her husband Bill Macy, won three Emmys. Everyone won but me. That night I had been nominated for two Emmys, for 'Door to Door' and 'The Roman Spring of Mrs Stone', but I didn't win anything.

One of the most romantic things I can think of is to have a private vaporetto in Venice to ferry you around. Here are my husband and my friend and assistant Sandy at the time of the screening of 'The Queen'.

Smile and answer the same question ten thousand times as if for the first time. And then do it all again for another project, and another…
Opposite: With Natasha, my nephew Simon's daughter, at the BAFTAs, 2007.

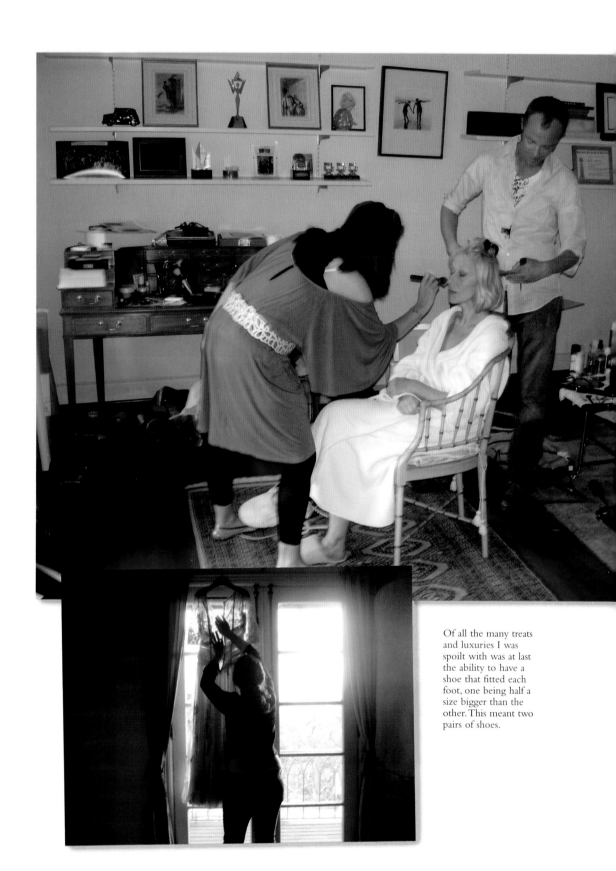

Of all the many treats and luxuries I was spoilt with was at last the ability to have a shoe that fitted each foot, one being half a size bigger than the other. This meant two pairs of shoes.

This was the first
(and probably the last) time I have had a real couture
dress made for me. Christian Lacroix designed it and his
lovely team of talented ladies came to London and fitted
the dress, and then on to LA to make sure that all was in
order. It was the most beautiful thing I had ever seen, as
gorgeous inside as out. I felt so comfortable and, at the
same time, so glamorous.

Left: With Kate
on the red carpet.
Below: The family
get to touch my little
gold man.

Oscar Acceptance Speech

Thank you Academy, thank you so much. A huge honour.
You know my sister told me that all kids love to get gold stars
and this is the biggest and the best gold star that I have
ever had in my life. I want to share my gold star with my
fellow nominees, those brilliant, brilliant actresses who gave such
amazing performances this year. I also share my gold star
with the film-makers, with Stephen Frears, with Peter
Morgan, with Andy Harries and all the producers and all
the film-makers and the cast. Thank you. Now you know
for fifty years and more Elizabeth Windsor has maintained
her dignity, her sense of duty and
her hair style. She's had her feet
planted firmly on the ground, her
hat on her head, her handbag on her
arm and she's weathered many, many
storms and I salute her courage and
her consistency and I thank her
because if it wasn't for her I most,
most certainly would not be here.
Ladies and Gentlemen I give you
the Queen! Thank you, thank you
very much.

# Taylor and My Family Today

## One wedding and a very happy clan

**For some reason**, even though my parents had a happy and successful marriage, I had no desire or ambition for marriage or children. I love children. I find them funny and inspiring. And I think people like my parents, who sacrifice personal freedom and economic wealth for the well-being and happiness of their children, are the true heroes of our society. But I just did not want that. I loved my life of freedom, and of work.

I also loved the men I had the good fortune to share my life with. They educated me about boxing and rock and roll and fell walking and dry-stone wall building and photography and sailing and gardening, and above all about how to love. They made me laugh and I think they loved me and I will forever be grateful for that. However I did not want to marry them.

I don't mean to be flippant, but I think a part of that was that I did not need to wear the dress. Maybe a lot of women get married because they are longing to wear that big white dress and the beautiful tiara, look lovely and get their make-up done. They crave to be the centre of attention for a day at least.

I had had the opportunity to experience all that by being an actress. I had beautiful dresses handmade for me, make-up done on me, people looking at me and so forth as a part of my profession. So that particular reason for getting married was not pertinent. I was also happy not to be particularly responsible to anyone or for anyone except my work and myself.

As soon as I was in my thirties, while giving interviews to promote a piece of work I had done, I found myself being asked about my marital status. It seemed a sexist question to me, as I don't think male actors were asked the same thing. I would always respond that I had nothing against marriage, it just wasn't for me. It was not that I didn't agree with marriage; but that, without being Catholic, I didn't agree with divorce. What I meant was that I simply could not see the point of being married if there was the remotest possibility of being divorced. I mean, what was the point? It was so easy and pleasurable to live together, and obviously such a pain to divorce. Besides, at that time marriage never seemed such a good deal for the woman involved.

In fact I had a recurring nightmare about getting married. I would be walking down the aisle, big dress, veil, church full of well-dressed people, knowing that in some hotel there was a vast, expensive banquet arranged, knowing it was a horrible mistake but not being brave enough to say so.

All my relationships took second place to my work, the fun of it and the intensity of it and my ambitions within it. I continued merrily along this path, having a series of relationships that had all the requirements of passion and lust and domesticity and tears and laughter and love, until I met Taylor. We met, as I have described, on the film *White Nights*. I was in my late thirties by then and he just a few months older.

It was certainly not love at first sight. After that meeting in Los Angeles, I would have taken a hefty bet against it if someone had suggested that this was the man I would complete my life with.

Firstly I had never had a relationship with a director in all my years of work. Somehow that was off limits to me. I could not see how to work properly under those conditions.

Also, more importantly, Taylor was married, with two children from two different marriages.

Visiting Taylor on the set.

But as soon as the film started, and then as it progressed, our attraction to each other became a clear and unavoidable force. Taylor's strength, which he shares with many film directors, is his positive nature, and his ability to press forward against all odds. One of his faults, albeit usually a charming one, is his precipitous nature. After a separation of six months or so, when I returned to Britain in the hope of putting some distance between the two of us, Taylor turned up in London. With much pain, he had separated from his wife. My fate was sealed.

My first years in Los Angeles as Taylor's partner were very difficult for me. Once he had made that complicated decision to take me on board, I felt that for the first time in my life I should put my relationship before my work. It was the least I could do. The geographical distance between our two homes and families meant something had to give if this was going to succeed, and I did not want yet another wonderful-but-only-four-years-long relationship.

Taylor had made major changes in his life for me, and I thought I should do the same. So I arrived in LA, was driven to our new, rented home in the Hollywood Hills, in which we were to live with Taylor's older son Rio, who was fifteen at the time, and then I was introduced to the very equitable Californian concept of joint custody as far as his second son Alex was concerned.

It was a whole new world for me, utterly alien and fraught with difficulty. I had no experience with children and I had absolutely no profile in Hollywood as an actress. In spite of my appearance in two Hollywood films, I was not even C list – if anything, I was Y list.

When Taylor took me to my first big 'studio head'-type Hollywood party, the tattoo on my left hand was suddenly a serious embarrassment. I told people I'd got it in prison when I was running with a bad crowd. They were suitably horrified that a risen star of Hollywood film-making had hooked up with such a creature. Nowadays of course they all have tattoos, but then it was a sign of total depravity.

The people who ultimately got me through the anxiety, the embarrassment and my feelings of awful displacement were Taylor's sons, Alex and Rio. They were always kind to me, and ultimately loving. They had grown up in a world I knew nothing about. They lived a life so very different from anything I had experienced as a child or even as an adult. My arrival in their world had caused upheaval and pain. Yet they gave me sympathy and courtesy from the beginning, and I loved them.

I also loved Taylor for putting his sons above me. I loved a man whose primary concern in life was his responsibility towards his children.

This does not mean that there were not difficult times. Often I wanted to give up and go back to where I was wanted. Work-wise, I could not get started. When I arrived, films were being made almost exclusively for the young teenage market, an audience that Hollywood had ignored for a while and recently rediscovered. There are never that many roles for women, and whatever roles I could have played inevitably went to actresses with a bigger Hollywood profile than me. I was at the back of the line, just like that time in primary school, except this time I couldn't even get the 'one of the twenty-four blackbirds' role.

At this point, Taylor did a memorable thing. I had gone to meet him for lunch at the Raleigh studios, where he was working. Crying, I started trying to explain all my difficulties. There was a path by the side of the studio that reached far into the distance. He took me to the beginning of this path, took two steps, and said 'Don't worry. Look, we are only this far along in our life together, we have all that way to go. Some will be hard and some will be easy, but we will make it.'

I think this was the moment I finally absolutely fell in love with him.

A few years later I was asked to do a play in LA, *A Woman in Mind* by Alan Ayckbourn. I had been asked to do other plays in America but had had to turn them down because I did not have the right visa (this was before I got my Green Card). This time, however, I could do the play because it was in an 'Equity Waiver' theatre with fewer than two hundred seats. I think the pay was two hundred dollars a week, but it was so good to have a job to go off to in the mornings. It's also a wonderful play.

One Wednesday morning as I went off to work, I heard on the television that the verdict in the trial of the police officers involved in the Rodney King beating was to be announced. When news of the acquittal broke, the city exploded. We were advised to stop rehearsals and go home. There was a palpable feeling of danger in the city. I have never known anything like it. A sixth sense told you not to go out.

I was on my own, as Taylor had gone to New Orleans for Jazz Fest. The next night from our house I could see in the distance fires breaking out in South Central. Every minute or so another fire would ignite in a billow of dark smoke. Taylor flew in that night, worried about me on my own in LA. I was so pleased to see him. We climbed the hill behind our house and watched as those fires moved inexorably towards the Hollywood Hills, closer and closer until they reached Hollywood Boulevard, just a few yards below our house. One of the last shops to be burned and looted was Frederick's of Hollywood on Hollywood Boulevard. When we could finally go out, a couple of days later, I drove by the store, one of my favourites in LA. It was completely empty. Every red frilly bustier, pink thong and fringed balcony bra was gone. I quite liked the idea of a terrifying South Central gangbanger running off with armloads of tarty women's underwear.

When *Prime Suspect* became a big hit in America, winning the coveted Emmy, my profile was raised a little. I was asked by Kevin Bacon and his wife Kyra Sedgwick to appear in a piece about a lesbian relationship called *Losing Chase*. Again I won an Emmy. This led to some of my work I like the best: *The Passion of Ayn Rand* and *The Roman Spring of Mrs Stone*, both of which were nominated, with *Ayn Rand* again winning me an Emmy. Sadly, none of these pieces has been shown in Britain.

In LA I experienced riots and earthquakes, fires and floods, in the way of that naturally dramatic city. Taylor and I were never Beverly Hills types; in fact I went for years without ever going to Rodeo Drive, or the beach, or anywhere west of La Cienega. We lived in old Hollywood, which at that time was the haunt of drug addicts and hookers. If we went out to dinner it would be in East Los Angeles, Mexican food being Taylor's favourite cuisine.

With the help of Alex and Rio, we grew to understand how to live together, and eventually to work parallel to each other, but we still did not get married for many years – fourteen, to be exact. Marriage was simply not a necessity for us. I had achieved the aim, impressed upon me by my mother, of being economically independent. I always kept my own home in London, and as the years went on most of my work was in Britain, while Taylor's was in America. Taylor always gave me the same freedom to work as I did him, and that of course is one of the many reasons we are still together.

Taylor can be turbulent, irrational and explosive. He has made me cry on many occasions. Coming from a family where voices were not often raised, the conflicts sometimes were unbearable. I am non-confrontational, a scaredy cat where that is concerned. Taylor has no fear of confrontation, which makes me cringe in British embarrassment.

He is also the most unsexist man, looking women directly in the eye with no curtain of assumptions or prejudices to cloud his view. He is brave, loyal and supportive. He is the man to turn to in an emergency, and he has been a wonderful mentor to many people. He is neither jealous of success nor impressed by it, although he enjoys and celebrates it. He is understanding of and sympathetic to failure. He also tried to teach me, not altogether successfully, not to be afraid of the phone.

In the end, and with our two families becoming very close, there was no longer any reason for us not to be married. And anyway the estate laws of both our countries preferred us to be married. So we decided to do it – and set a date a mere six weeks away. Then I sat back and my director husband-to-be took over.

A few years earlier we had enjoyed a wonderful Hogmanay in Scotland with Alex and Rio, who had been introduced to the delights of single malt whisky and Scottish reels. Taylor has Scottish roots, being a McAllister on his mother's side. Also his birthday is on 31st December. So we came up with the idea of celebrating the New Year, his birthday and our marriage all in one day.

We found a castle for rent: Castle Stuart, a medieval structure with fairy-tale turrets. The Stuart family, who run it, were the very best of hosts. With sixteen of our closest friends and family we spent the most fabulous four days leading up to the wedding in those magical surroundings.

The wedding took place in a small and simple church in Ardersier, a little fishing village near Inverness. As I arrived, kindly driven by Charles Stuart in his old Bentley, there was a crowd of people from the village outside the church. They had heard about the wedding, probably through the florist, who lived in the village. I invited them all to come in if they wanted. As I walked down the aisle, I could hear the crowd quietly coming in behind me. Alex White, the vicar, who was very shy but welcoming, waited until everyone was in and then announced, 'We are here to witness the marriage of Helen to Taylor, but first I would like to tell you all that it is Taylor's birthday today and I think we should all sing him "Happy Birthday"!' Whereupon Taylor's family, with the people of Ardersier, did just that.

Later we saw in the New Year in the Scottish tradition by banging on saucepans outside, and dancing and drinking until the small wee hours.

My Dear Mum

Writing that addess sounds so full of sunshine and normally it is

but today the rain is pouring down and it is a very welcome sight, especially

for the poor parched soil that has to be painstakingly and expensively watered

more or less every day. But when it rains here it just teems down like a grey

curtain. However before I left I had indeed been watering the sad dried up

roses that I held no hope for but watered all the same, and when I got back

a miracle had occurred! beautiful pink roses, profusions of them, on lovely

green leaves had shot up so fast that they had done the whole thing in just

10 days or so. Plants are amazing sometimes in their resilience and ability

to respond to care, although I'm sure you dont agree in the case of petunias.

Infact I have bought some petunias and put them in and they are behaving just

like yours! Perhaps it is a family failing

This  big house was great to come home to although I'm sure when you eventually

see it you will think it much too big to ever be homely, but in fact it is

It will be quite some time before ti is all redecorated but in the meantime

it is perfectly livable in. And I am living in it as a complete lady of leisure

having my nails done and reading the paper. Iwould of course much prefer to

be working but it looks as if the work that I was going to do in New York

(Strindberg at the Public Theater which is the New York equivalent of the

Royal Court only bigger ind better) is going to fall through on account of

immigration/ equity problems which basically means that the union are saying

why let an english actress do it when ther are so many unemployed american

actresses. It is a rat because I really wanted to do that peice of work and

the theatre really wanted me to as well. Oh well, part and parcel of the

struggle. All else here is fine. Rio is in trouble today because he missed

a lesson at school today and was found out and from what I remember about

that kind of feeling its worse than being turned down by equity. He is sitting

in his room waiting to be told off by his dad. The trouble is his dad was a very high achiever at school and also very keen, I mean he actually enjoyed school! So it is difficult for him to understand someone who hates it, especially if he is paying for it.

In my next letter to you I will send pictures of this mansion and the roses!

All my love to you for now

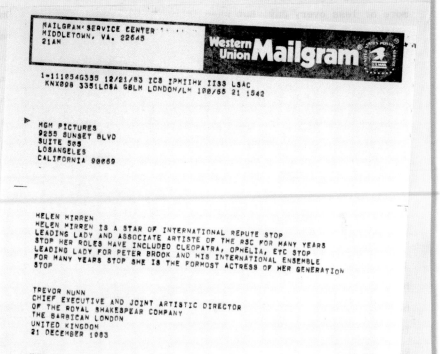

MAILGRAM SERVICE CENTER
MIDDLETOWN, VA. 22645
21AM

Western Union Mailgram

1-111054G355 12/21/83 ICS IPMIIHK IISS LSAC
KNX098 3351LOSA GBLM LONDON/LM 100/65 21 1542

MGM PICTURES
9255 SUNSET BLVD
SUITE 505
LOSANGELES
CALIFORNIA 90069

HELEN MIRREN
HELEN MIRREN IS A STAR OF INTERNATIONAL REPUTE STOP
LEADING LADY AND ASSOCIATE ARTISTE OF THE RSC FOR MANY YEARS
STOP HER ROLES HAVE INCLUDED CLEOPATRA, OPHELIA, ETC STOP
LEADING LADY FOR PETER BROOK AND HIS INTERNATIONAL ENSEMBLE
FOR MANY YEARS STOP SHE IS THE FORMOST ACTRESS OF HER GENERATION
STOP

TREVOR NUNN
CHIEF EXECUTIVE AND JOINT ARTISTIC DIRECTOR
OF THE ROYAL SHAKESPEAR COMPANY
THE BARBICAN LONDON
UNITED KINGDOM
21 DECEMBER 1983

NNN

11141 EST

MGMCOMP

*Here is a letter written to my mother when I first got to America and began my adventure with Taylor and his sons. I am glad to see that I do not mention that I was crying every day because I felt so out of place. To get my Green Card to work in the theatre in America, I had to show that I was a proper actress. It took a whole heap of letters like this one from Trevor Nunn.*

This is a page of my favourite pictures of my special, remarkable husband. He always wears red on the set as he likes the crew to be easily able to see him. He is also typically American and always on the phone. I must have a thousand pictures like these.

THURSDAY JANUARY 1 1998

DRINK OR DRIVE
Is one glass too many?
Mary Ann Sieghart
PAGE 16

UP FOR THE CUP
Zola on a Chelsea mission
PAGE 23

Helen Mirren at her marriage yesterday in Ardersier, Scotland to Taylor Hackford, an American film director

## Highland wedding for Helen Mirren

BY KATHRYN KNIGHT

THE actress Helen Mirren, who for many years has been an outspoken opponent of marriage, yesterday married her long-term partner in a small Highland church.

Villagers in the tiny parish of Ardersier, near Inverness, were invited to join the small band of guests who gathered to watch Miss Mirren, 51, tie the knot with the American director Taylor Hackford in

Above left: Here we are coming back to the castle from the church. Natasha was my bridesmaid. We were piped back into the castle. The Stuarts made a beautiful wedding for us.
Above right: *The Times*.
Opposite: George, my ex, and Taylor's best friend, Tony, look on as I show how very happy I am.

*My wedding jacket came from the 70 per cent off sale rail in a store in LA. The skirt came from somewhere else. My husband gave me the lovely baroque pearls.*

| DOLPHIN INTERNATIONAL TRAVEL Tel: 0171-834 0394 | | | | | | ITINERARY |
|---|---|---|---|---|---|---|
| DATE | JOURNEY | FLIGHT | DEPARTS | ARRIVES | ALLOWANCE klg | REMARKS |
| 29th Dec 97 | Euston - Inverness | TRAIN SLEEPER | 21.30 | 08.40* | Coach H - | Berth 09 |
| 02nd Jan 98 | Inverness - Gatwick | BA 2987 | 17.30 | 19.10 | 1 piece | |
| | | | | | | |
| | * arrival the next day | | | | | |

BEFORE <u>21.00</u> HOURS

Inverness Airport before <u>17.00</u> hours

OF SIX MONTHS.

Above: We all took the sleeper train from London to Scotland for the wedding, having to change trains at 5.30 a.m. The first train was late, so all of us had to run down the platform in a panic. We only made it because the rail employees kindly held the second train for us. Middle: Here I am happily signing away my freedom, with the help of my beloved sister, and my stepson, Rio. And two cousins-in-law who are like brothers: Rio and Simon. Taylor made his sons wear kilts in honour of their Scottish ancestry. Rio managed to make it look very fashionable … He is wearing his Las Vegas dice belt. Below: Before the marriage, with my good Parsenn Sally friends, Sandy Campbell and Sarah Ponsonby.

The spectacular castle
and the simple little
church that was the
scene of my wedding.

My family now consists of my husband, Taylor, the president of us all; my sister, the queen of us all; her son Simon, his wife Louise, and his children, Natasha, Cameron and Felix; my brother Peter's son Basil; and Taylor's sons, my stepsons, Alex and Rio. Lots of boys, and my very happiest moments are when I am together with all of them, which happens quite often.

They all get on really well. Simon, my beloved surrogate son, is now a successful writer in Hollywood. Alex also works in Los Angeles, in the music and video game world, and Rio has become a music and bar entrepreneur, with successful bars in New Orleans and San Francisco. Basil works in the film business in the camera department and is a young director of photography. Natasha is still in school in Cannes, where she lives with her mother, and Cameron and Felix are on their way to becoming the LA boys that their grown-up step-cousins are. We are an international family, with deep roots on both sides of the Atlantic. I am often asked where I consider to be home, and really I have no answer for that. I am first and foremost a London Girl, an Essex Girl even, but my home is wherever this motley clan of Scottish/English (Taylor), Scottish/Jewish (Alex and Rio), Russian/English (Kate and I), Irish/Russian/English (Basil), and Welsh/Russian/English (Simon), Jewish/English (Louise), Welsh/Jewish/Russian/English (Cameron and Felix), and Russian/English/Irish/French (Natasha), all of us with a bit of French thrown in as well, collect, and become as one.

Far left: My nephew Simon's eldest son, Cameron. Clockwise from top: my sister Kate; My favourite picture of all our boys together, only little Felix is missing, not yet born. It was taken in the kitchen of my house in London, Christmas 2004 – Simon, Alex, Basil and Rio with Cameron; Natasha as a little cutie, wearing my wedding skirt and lying across another very old member of my family, the leopard that James gave me as a birthday present many years ago; two photographs of little Felix; my nephew Simon and his wife Louise.

Top: Taylor, me, Alex and
Rio at the house in LA.
Above right: Kate, cousin
Tania and me.
Above left: Taylor, Kate,
Louise and Simon visiting
me backstage.

Clockwise from top:
Cameron was very
excited and pleased to
have a brother and has
miraculously stayed that
way; my proud sister and
her second grandchild
whom I get to borrow;
Taylor wants his own
grandchildren but is
happy to borrow as well;
my favourite photo with
Taylor, Alex and Rio;
Simon with baby Natasha,
both sleeping.

# Professional Shots

**I have always found it** hard to go by an automatic photo booth without going in to take some silly pictures. I persuade whoever I am with to participate… It's better with other people.

Here I am then, with James Wedge, with Janet Suzman, on my own a few times, with James Mason, with Rio and Taylor. One of the reasons I love these booths is that they capture a tiny moment in time. The process takes seconds, the result instantaneous.

I have been photographed many times since I was nineteen. In the course of my professional life I have been shot by some very famous photographers, some real artists, some iconoclastic photographers and by some simply very good professional photographers – and let's not forget the terrible hacks, of which there have also been a few. The hacks always call you 'dear', which makes me want to head-butt them. I have been photographed for magazines, newspapers, and press releases. Ultimately, it is a part of my work. It comes under the heading of publicity, and no matter what work you do, whether it is in a small theatre seating two hundred or a film destined for an international release, or a television piece hopefully to be seen by millions, it is a part of your job to make the audience aware of the project. In other words, to get the bums on the seats. You do this by speaking to publications, and with the words go the pictures. I try to approach this side of my work with professionalism and understanding.

This kind of photography is very controlled and time consuming. At one of the shoots shown here, I counted twenty people on the set – all to take one picture of me. Every single person except myself had at least one assistant. The photographer had five. They never used the picture. Of course it's not always like that. That was an extreme example.

Sometimes it presents a fantasy, sometimes it is a genuine attempt at portraiture, but it always takes a lot of time and energy. I have enjoyed working with photographers, and, since my relationship with James Wedge, I've given them the time and respect they need. Here is a small part of our work together.

Opposite, top: James Wedge and I; right, Janet Suzman and I; on my own a few times.
Above: with James Mason.
Right: with Rio and Taylor.

I have worked with Tony Snowdon three times.
He is an extraordinarily precise photographer,
knowing exactly the image he wishes to capture.
He is also great fun to be with.

Taken by Lord Snowdon in the 1970s.

The picture opposite is the result of one of the many photo sessions I had to do through the release of 'The Queen'. It was shot in New York, and the photographer graffitied parts of my thank you speech from the Oscars on the wall behind me. I love all the contrasts.

Below: I can't remember who took this photograph but I do remember that I was running late and needed a bath...

Opposite: I loved this
dress and set up this
shoot myself to show
it off in all its glory.

This was the shoot that I counted at least
twenty people on set to take just the one shot
of me. It was never used.

Opposite: A photo-
graph by Julian Broad.
Right: A shot taken by
Rankin.

I love the idea of extreme photography -
trying something different and giving yourself
over to the unique style of the photographer.
The photographs on this page are the work
of two of my favourite photographers. I like
to give photographers complete freedom in their
work. That way with inventive and creative
photographers you get an arresting and sometimes
revealing image.

# Acknowledgements

**I thank the collaboration** of many friends: Sandy Campbell who goosed me into the project in the beginning and kept me going with her enthusiasm. The picture editor of the book, Chris Worwood, without whom this book would not exist. His patience, calm and organisation were invaluable. My family, who have tolerated me with good humour. Will Stewart for finding my family pictures in Russia. And finally all the friends from my life who helped by supplying pictures. I thank them for keeping the pictures in the first place: Kate Mirren, James Wedge, Mary Ellen Mark, Valentina Zimina, Sarah Ponsonby, Ken Cranham, George Galitzine, Jean Louis Alpeyrie, Jenni May.

I also thank all the photographers I have worked with over the years. Each one is singular in their approach and constantly re-invents the art of photography.

I thank Michael Dover for his expertise and wisdom. He is the midwife who brought this bawling child into the world of publishing. Also everyone at Orion and in particular Alan Samson for their patience and support.

And I would like to thank the Queen… Sorry, force of habit!

# Film

| | |
|---|---|
| 2005 | *The Queen* |
| | *Shadowboxer* |
| | *The Hitchhiker's Guide to the Galaxy* (voice) |
| 2004 | *The Clearing* |
| | *Raising Helen* |
| | *Pride* (voice) |
| 2002 | *Calender Girls* |
| 2001 | *Gosford Park* |
| | *No Such Thing* |
| | *Last Orders* |
| | *The Pledge* |
| | *Greenfingers* |
| 1999 | *Teaching Miss Tingle* |
| | *The Passion of Ayn Rand* |
| 1998 | *The Prince of Egypt* (voice) |
| 1997 | *Painted Lady* |
| | *Critical Care* |
| 1996 | *Some Mother's Son* |
| | *Losing Chase* |
| 1995 | *The Snow Queen* (voice) |
| 1994 | *The Prince of Jutland* |
| | *The Madness of King George* |
| 1993 | *The Hawk* |
| 1991 | *Where Angels Fear to Tread* |
| 1990 | *The Comfort of Strangers* |
| | *Bethune: The Making of a Hero* |
| 1989 | *Red King, White Knight* |
| | *The Cook, The Thief, His Wife and Her Lover* |
| | *Pascalis Island* |
| 1988 | *When the Whales Came* |
| 1987 | *Cause Célèbre* |
| 1986 | *The Mosquito Coast* |
| 1985 | *Coming Through* |
| 1985 | *Gospel According to Vic* |
| | *White Nights* |
| 1984 | *2010: The Year We Made Contact* |
| | *Cal* |
| 1983 | *Cymbeline* |
| 1981 | *A Midsummer Nights Dream* |
| | *Excalibur* |

| | |
|---|---|
| 1980 | *The Long Good Friday* |
| | *Caligula* |
| | *The Fiendish Plot of Fu Manchu* |
| | *Hussy* |
| 1978 | *As You Like It* |
| 1976 | *Hamlet* |
| 1975 | *The Collection* |
| 1973 | *O Lucky Man!* |
| 1972 | *Savage Messiah* |
| | *Miss Julie* |
| 1969 | *Age of Consent* |
| 1968 | *A Midsummers Nights Dream* |
| 1967 | *Herostratus* |

# Theatre

| | |
|---|---|
| 2003 | *Mourning Becomes Electra* |
| 2001 | *Dance of Death* |
| 2000 | *Orpheus Descending* |
| 1999 | *Collected Stories* |
| 1998 | *Antony and Cleopatra* |
| 1994 | *A Month in the Country* |
| 1991 | *Sex Please, We're Italian* |
| 1989 | *Two-Way Mirror* |
| 1988 | *Richard III* |
| 1987 | *Madam Bovary* |
| 1984 | *The Roaring Girl* |
| | *Extremities* |
| 1982 | *Antony and Cleopatra* |
| 1981 | *The Faith Healer* |
| 1980 | *The Duchess of Malfi* |
| 1979 | *Measure for Measure* |
| 1977 | *Henry VI* |
| 1975 | *The Seagull* |
| | *Teeth'n'Smiles* |
| | *The Bed Before Yesterday* |
| 1974 | *Macbeth* |
| 1971 | *Man of Mode* |
| | *Enemies* |
| 1970 | *Hamlet* |
| | *Two Gentlemen of Verona* |
| 1969 | *The Revenger's Tragedy* |
| | *Bartholomew Fair* |
| 1968 | *Troilus and Cressida* |
| | *Much Ado About Nothing* |
| 1967 | *The Silver Tassle* |
| | *All's Well That Ends Well* |
| 1966 | *Hamlet* |
| 1965 | *Antony and Cleopatra* |

# Television

| | |
|---|---|
| 2006 | *Prime Suspect 7* |
| 2005 | *Elizabeth I* |
| 2003 | *Prime Suspect 6* |
| 2002 | *The Roman Spring of Mrs Stone* |
| | *Georgetown* |
| | *Door to Door* |
| 2001 | *Terror in America* (narrator) |
| | *Boston Law* (narrator) |
| | *Happy Birthday* (director) |
| 2000 | *Long Night's Journey Into Day* (narrator) |
| 1999 | *French and Saunders* |
| | *Helen Mirren in South Africa* |
| 1997 | *Painted Lady* |
| 1996 | *Prime Suspect 5* |
| | *Losing Chase* |
| | *French and Saunders* |
| 1995 | *Prime Suspect 4 (Scent of Darkness; Inner Circles; The Lost Child)* |
| 1993 | *Prime Suspect 3* |
| | *The Hidden Room* |
| 1992 | *Prime Suspect 2* |
| 1990 | *Prime Suspect* |
| 1989 | *After the Party* |
| 1988 | *People of the Forest: The Chimps of Gombe* (narrator) |
| 1987 | *Invocation Maya Deren* (narrator) |
| 1982 | *Soft Targets* |
| 1981 | *Mrs Reinhardt* |
| 1979 | *The Serpent Son* |
| | *Blue Remembered Hills* |
| 1977 | *The Country Wife* |
| 1975 | *The Philanthropist* |
| | *The Apple Cart* |
| | *Caesar and Claretta* |
| | *The Empty Space* |
| | *The Little Minister* |
| 1974 | *A Coffin for the Bride* |
| | *The Changling* |
| | *Bellamira* |
| 1972 | *Cousin Bette* |

# Photo Credits

The publishers would like to thank the following sources for their kind permission to reproduce the photographs and illustrations in this book. Every effort has been made to contact the copyright holders, but we would be happy to correct any errors or omissions in future editions.

1 James Wedge; 2 John Swanell; 4–5 (Harlequin) James Wedge, (Prime Suspect) ITV PLC (Granada), (Elizabeth 1) Giles Keyte/Channel 4; 7 Giles Keyte; 35 EMPICS; 61 (top) Michael William; 82 (centre) Kenneth Cranham Private Collection; 89 John Goldblatt/ Daily Telegraph; 91 Sandy Campbell; 93 Paul Anmigen/Sunday Times; 97 (top left) REX Features; 98 (bottom) The Moviestore Collection; 102 (Top and middle) John Goldblatt/Daily Telegraph; 103 (top) Lindy Jones, (bottom) Sandy Campbell; 104–105 George Galitzine; 106 Colin Jones; 107 George Galitzine; 111 George Galitzine; 120–121 Mary Ellen Mark; 125 (Centre right) George Galitzine; 134 (bottom left) Getty Images; 135 Printed in The Guardian; 137 Time Out; 138–139 Steve Macmillan/The Observer, Ashton Radcliffe; 140 (top) Terry Smith/ Time Inc.; 141 Getty Images; 142-3 EMPICS; 143 (bottom) Shakespeare Birthplace Trust; 145 Corbis; 146 Abaca/EMPICS; 147 Getty Images; 148-9 Ashton Radcliffe; 153-169 James Wedge; 173 (middle) Corbis, (bottom) REX Features; 174 (top and bottom) REX Features, (middle) The Moviestore Collection; 178 (bottom) Corbis; 187 Carinthia West; 192-193 James Wedge; 194 EMPICS; 195 (top) REX Features, (bottom left) Corbis, (bottom right) AKG-Images; 196-199 Helen Mirren Private Collection and The Taylor Hackford Archive; 201-203 ITV PLC (Granada); 204 (top) REX Features; 207 REX Features; 208 Snowdon/ Camera Press; 209 (top) Alex Bailey; 210 EMPICS; 211 Courtesy of Universal Studios Licensing LLLP; 212 (top and bottom) The Moviestore Collection, (middle) Corbis; 214-215 REX Features; 219 Giles Keyte/Channel 4; 222 REX Features; 223 ITV PLC (Granada); 224-227 Giles Keyte/Channel 4; 229 REX Features; 241 REX Features; 250 (top and bottom left) Sandy Campbell; Sunday Times; 251 Sarah Ponsonby; 252 (Bottom) George Galitzine; 260-261 Snowdon/Camera Press; 263 Robert Earlman for Glamour Magazine; 266 Julian Broad; 267 Rankin.
All other images: Helen Mirren Private Collection.

First published in Great Britain in 2007 by Weidenfeld & Nicolson

10 9 8 7 6 5 4 3 2 1

Text © Helen Mirren 2007
Design and layout © Weidenfeld & Nicolson 2007

All rights reserved. No part of this publication may be reproduced, stored in a retrieval system, or transmitted, in any form or by any means, electronic, mechanical, photocopying, recording or otherwise, without the prior permission of both the copyright owners and the above publisher.

The right of the copyright holders to be identified as the authors of this work has been asserted in accordance with the Copyright, Designs and Patents Act 1988.

A CIP catalogue record for this book is available from the British Library.

ISBN: 978 0 297 85197 4

Design director: David Rowley
Design: Clive Hayball
Design assistance: Justin Hunt
Picture research: Brónagh Woods
Editorial: Lucinda McNeile, Anne O'Brien, Debbie Woska, Ilsa Yardley

Colour reproduction by DL Interactive
Printed and bound in Italy by Printer Trento and LEGO

Weidenfeld & Nicolson
The Orion Publishing Group Ltd
Orion House
5 Upper St Martin's Lane
London WC2H 9EA

An Hachette Livre UK Company

The Orion Publishing Group's policy is to use papers that are natural, renewable and recyclable products and made from wood grown in sustainable forests. The logging and manufacturing processes are expected to conform to the environmental regulations of the country of origin.